Praise for

YOUR QUANTUM BREAKTHROUGH CODE

"Once again, Sandra Anne Taylor has written a powerful book. It can help anyone decode negative patterns in their life—and then it shows you how to encode positive, empowering patterns. It's simple, it's effective . . . and anyone can do it. Highly recommended!"

— DENISE LINN,
international best-selling author of
Unlock the Secret Messages of Your Body!

"No matter where you are on your journey—or how spiritual you are—there is always room for self-reflection and taking time to look in the mirror and break the mold. I have found this book to be truly brilliant, inspiring, informative, and transformational. It's certainly a book that everyone needs to read, and you will refer back to it again and again. If you don't think you can change . . . think again. You will break the code!"

— LISA WILLIAMS,
international best-selling author of *The Survival of the Soul*

"Imagine if you could be released from the old ways of thinking. What if you could learn something so profound that your life would be changed forever? What if the fates gave you the codes to find everlasting joy and success? How fortunate would that be? Well, Sandra Anne Taylor's book **Your Quantum Breakthrough Code** gives you those codes and much more. Most important, her book gives you simple techniques that make it possible for you to create and sustain a life that is in total alignment with your destiny. Change your life by discovering **Your Quantum Breakthrough Code.** You owe it to yourself."

— CAROL RITBERGER, PH.D.,
author of *What Color Is Your Personality?*

"Sandra Anne Taylor has done it once again with **Your Quantum Breakthrough Code.** Sandra is a master teacher and has distilled her brilliant understanding of the mind, intention, and consciousness into a simple and beautiful process for turning negative thinking and limiting beliefs into your heart's fullest desires and potential. The great thing is that it's easy and fun—and best of all, it works. I love this book and the beautiful process it teaches!"

— DR. DARREN R. WEISSMAN,
developer of The LifeLine Technique

YOUR QUANTUM BREAK-THROUGH CODE

ALSO BY SANDRA ANNE TAYLOR

Books

*Quantum Success: The Astounding Science of
Wealth and Happiness**

*Secrets of Success: The Science and Spirit of
Real Prosperity,* with Sharon A. Klingler*

*Secrets of Attraction: The Universal Laws of
Love, Sex, and Romance**

Truth, Triumph, and Transformation:
Sorting Out the Fact from the Fiction in Universal Law*

28 Days to a More Magnetic Life*

The Hidden Power of Your Past Lives:
Revealing Your Encoded Consciousness*

The Energy Oracle Cards: 53 Card Deck and Guidebook*

Guided Visualizations, CDs, and Audio Programs

Energy Breakthrough Meditations, including:
*Power Chakra Clearing, Rescripting Beliefs,
Clearing the Road Ahead,* and
Affirmations for Self-Empowerment

Act to Attract (nine-CD audio seminar and workbook)

Act to Attract Meditations, including: *Attracting Love,
Your Sacred Identity,* and *Morning and Evening Affirmations* (CD)

Attracting Success, including: *Attracting Success
and Planting Your Destiny Garden,*
and *Mystic Journey Music* (CD)

Healing Journeys, including: *Cellular Regression:
Timeless Healing* and *Relaxation and Memory Release* (CD)

*Available from Hay House

Please visit:

Hay House USA: www.hayhouse.com®
Hay House Australia: www.hayhouse.com.au
Hay House UK: www.hayhouse.co.uk
Hay House South Africa: www.hayhouse.co.za
Hay House India: www.hayhouse.co.in

YOUR QUANTUM BREAK- THROUGH CODE

The Simple Technique That Brings Everlasting Joy and Success

Sandra Anne Taylor

HAY HOUSE, INC.
Carlsbad, California • New York City
London • Sydney • Johannesburg
Vancouver • Hong Kong • New Delhi

Published and distributed in the United States by: Hay House, Inc.: www
.hayhouse.com® • *Published and distributed in Australia by:* Hay House
Australia Pty. Ltd.: www.hayhouse.com.au • *Published and distributed
in the United Kingdom by:* Hay House UK, Ltd.: www.hayhouse.co.uk •
Published and distributed in the Republic of South Africa by: Hay House
SA (Pty), Ltd.: www.hayhouse.co.za • *Distributed in Canada by:* Raincoast
Books: www.raincoast.com • *Published in India by:* Hay House Publishers
India: www.hayhouse.co.in

Cover design: Amy Rose Grigoriou • *Interior design:* Pamela Homan
Interior illustrations: Joanna Van Rensselaer

The author of this book does not dispense medical advice or pre-
scribe the use of any technique as a form of treatment for physical, emotional, or medical problems without the advice of a physician, either
directly or indirectly. The intent of the author is only to offer information
of a general nature to help you in your quest for emotional and spiritual
well-being. In the event you use any of the information in this book for
yourself, the author and the publisher assume no responsibility for your
actions.

Cataloging-in-Publication Data is on file with the Library of Congress

Tradepaper ISBN: 978-1-4019-4045-4

10 9 8 7 6 5 4 3 2 1
1st edition, November 2014

SUSTAINABLE
FORESTRY
INITIATIVE
Certified Chain of Custody
Promoting Sustainable Forestry
www.sfiprogram.org
SFI-01268

SFI label applies to the text stock

Printed in the United States of America

*This book is dedicated to
my dear, beloved friends
Candace B. Pert
and
Michele Jacob.
I miss you both so much!*

CONTENTS

INTRODUCTION

THE VOICE IN THE DREAM

"When the state of dreaming has dawned,
do not lie in ignorance like a corpse.
Enter the natural sphere of unwavering attentiveness.
Recognize your dreams and
transform illusion into luminosity."

— **Tibetan Buddhist Prayer**

This book is an extremely personal and exciting project for me, perhaps because of the way I received the key information. Some people may find this crazy or just a little hard to believe, but I'm determined to be nakedly honest about the entire experience.

The truth is, I was given the specific information about the decoding and coding techniques in a dream. Some people might say the information was "channeled" to me. Others might say that after 25 years of studying quantum physics and neuroscience, the information somehow just coalesced in my subconscious mind. I myself think it was a gift from Spirit, although I don't know from whom. Perhaps it was a guide, a healing angel, or the Divine Consciousness that so generously gave this information to me. I may never know, but whomever it was, I will be eternally grateful—both for the changes this technique has made in my life and for the amazing transformations I've seen it bring to others. And now, although it feels a little risky because it's so very different, I want to share both the information and the experience with you.

Dreaming Big

A few years ago, I was working with a client named Peggy who was having a difficult time breaking through some old patterns of self-doubt and self-criticism. Of course, this significantly affected her happiness, but it also affected her career experience as well. We had been using affirmations and meditations with very good results in several areas of her life, but she kept hitting a wall where her confidence in her career was concerned. She was continually tense at meetings, always feeling she appeared inadequate and incapable in other people's eyes.

I thought about her often, longing to ease her sadness and frustration. As I was falling asleep one night, I found that she was once again on my mind. I said—to no one in particular—"There must be something I'm missing. There must be something *easy* that she can do to break through this terrorizing habit of self-doubt."

That night I had a dream that was as clear as if I were in a waking state. Although I didn't see anybody, a male voice spoke to me, giving me step-by-step directions for the decoding and coding process you will find in this book. His voice was strong yet gentle, loving yet firm, educational and compassionate all at the same time. He was detailed about how the position should be held and how the statements should be worded. At the end of the dream, he said, *Use this yourself. Teach it to Peggy—and to all.*

When I woke up, I immediately wrote down everything I had learned in the dream. The process seemed too simple to be that effective, but I detailed it step-by-step. And I did what I was told—I started using it myself and also taught it to Peggy. She's a different person now, and the in-depth story of her profound transformation is told later in the book.

In the few years since that dream, I have taught this technique to many clients and at a number of seminars, and I have used it myself with amazing results. In fact, it's astounding how much happier I am since starting to do this process on a regular basis. I've always tended to be pretty happy, but like so many others, I find that my experience of joy can be easily derailed by the little things in life. So I do the coding whenever I'm feeling stressed, under a deadline, worried about the kids, or even just sad about some new suffering in faraway places. When such things take me out of my heart, I simply do the coding process, and although the external concerns may not have changed, my inner consciousness—and my emotions—certainly do.

Looking Ahead

This book is divided into five sections, the order of which is designed to give background and preparation for the coding technique itself.

Part I relates some personal experiences showing the power of the coding technique. It also examines the science of mind and energy behind the process. This background is important because it reveals the critical principles of change and energetic transformation involved.

Part II is a detailed look at the four steps necessary to initiate the Quantum Breakthrough Code. This is a crucial part of the preparation process, so let yourself follow the suggestions outlined there.

Part III is the Quantum Breakthrough Code itself. This technique combines the decoding process and the coding process, which have slightly different positions. (The images that show those positions are in Chapters 8 and 9.) There are some sample statements to get you started and answers to the most common questions regarding this technique, along with suggestions for employing this process to create the happiest, most fulfilling life possible.

Part IV, The Seven Breakthrough Forces, takes you even further into the process. It explores the dynamic powers that are always available but often dismissed in our striving for happiness. Yet each of these forces can give immeasurable assistance in that pursuit.

This section also investigates the blocks that keep people stuck in their same old frustrations. This investigation is vital for the decoding part of the process. Each chapter offers coding points, suggested statements to be used during the process itself.

The book closes with Part V, which will help you move forward using your new tools, creating lasting success and happiness in your life!

The Happiness Factor

By now I'm sure you're wondering what the coding technique is. This profoundly life-changing process is actually a simple technique that engages a certain position, placing your fingertips on your forehead and using directive statements. This may sound extremely simplistic, but there is purpose and meaning behind the method. The breakthrough code helps release unwanted patterns and establish new energetic directions. In essence, it reorganizes your inner nature in healthy and conscious ways.

This book is designed to help you break through the blocks in your life, and the first step is identifying the old, rigid stuff that's been keeping you stuck. Whatever self-sabotaging pattern that needs to be dismantled can be decoded. Then you can build a prosperous and happy life based on a new consciousness code that is free, joyous, and self-empowered.

You see, most of us live in an unconscious, reactionary mode, which is directed by some deeply encrypted codes that we are not even aware of. As a result, we keep experiencing the same difficult emotions, projecting the same energy, and getting the same old results. It's important to find out what these hidden codes are and how they influence our lives.

So let yourself do some honest investigation. Find out what's stopping you and how you can arrive at a new code of freedom, happiness, and empowerment that becomes your central viewpoint. Your happiness and freedom are vital components of your energetic connection with the Universe. This is another reason why the coding process is so important. Understanding your energy and how it resonates with the world around you is a profoundly liberating process. All things change when you direct your process with purpose—and your use of the coding technique is a very purposeful activity.

Every single time you code happiness and feel a shift in your consciousness, you will also shift into a more magnetic resonance with the people, situations, and the world around you. When you decode attachment, fear, and negativity, you create a new code that is clear and vibrant, flowing freely within you and from you into the great field of all possibilities—where synchronicity and unknown blessings always abide.

The best use of this process is to make it a way of life. Although several people have reported major transformations after just a few weeks, the ideal approach is to establish the coding technique as a part of your daily routine. Switching old codes of thought and emotion can actually redirect nervousness into peace and dissatisfaction into joy. And isn't that the way you want to live your life forever?

There's a very specific plan for the elements in this book. The power of this technique is impressive, but it will be even more so if it is comprehensively approached. *You are worth every moment of the time and energy you put into this process.* After all, it's your life, your happiness, and your genuine freedom in the mix. Follow the recipe, and you will be delighted by the feast you find!

Your Own Inner Power Line

You have powerful *breakthrough forces* within that, when awakened, can shift your reality in dramatic ways. These wonderful energetic patterns are already vibrating through your history and your eternal life. Each of these forces is a generator of strong and focused personal and Universal energy, and each can be ignited to spark profound inner joy.

Each of the seven breakthrough forces examined in Part IV corresponds with one of your primary energy centers, or chakras, and each one holds incredible power and profoundly healing and liberating codes that could be lying dormant within. *To help awaken these forces fully in your life, it's important to examine each of these powerful quantum factors in three key ways.*

The Influence of the Breakthrough Forces

1. **The power of the force itself**—what it is and how awakening it can enhance your life experience.

2. **The ignitors of each powerful force,** which are the activities that you can engage in to accelerate the manifestation of these radiant vibrations. When you live your life consciously, your consciousness creation shines!

3. **The reactive patterns and negative codes that could be blocking that force,** preventing your happiness and locking up the energy center where each force resides. It's important to be open and honest with yourself about the negative habits you've gotten into. Let yourself be willing to take a good hard look at those things you want to change. By decoding the unhealthy inner patterns that just seem to keep holding on, you will be able to break through the unwanted outer blocks that stop you from moving forward.

It's *your* life that you're living, and only you can do something about it. If there's anything at all that you would like to change, you can take charge now. You're going to get from here to the future anyway, so you might as well use this time to take the steps that will move you in the direction that you desire.

Your Coding Journal

Don't let the simplicity of the coding process fool you; this is a very serious and life-changing endeavor. As with any journey, it is helpful to figure out where you are now, and to determine where you want to go. One thing that you can do to help this process along is to keep a coding journal.

This book is designed to help you clearly investigate your present patterns and plan your future desired direction. It is inestimably helpful to keep a record of your responses to the material in each chapter and impressions of your decoding and coding practices. Here are some suggestions for doing your journal work:

- As you read about the breakthrough forces, write down some affirmations and intentions to integrate their power into your life.

- Notice how you can implement each of the force's ignitors; make a plan to engage in these activities little by little each day.

- While studying the reactive patterns, jot down any that you may recognize in yourself. Make it a clear intention to decode even the most deeply held or difficult response.

- As you go through the sections titled Coding Points, make sure you notice which statements resonate with you the most. Underline them in the book, or write them down in your coding journal. You can also use these—or variations of these—as affirmations until you become more comfortable with the techniques and positions described in Chapters 8 and 9.

It will also be important to use your journal to vent any uncomfortable emotion that may come up—even if it's buried in some distant past event. Many of our very negative codes are sourced in some extremely traumatic experiences. The coding technique is not designed to just dismiss or deny that. Use your journal, and if you find there's something deeper to deal with, let yourself seek the help of a professional—one who resonates with you and who is supportive to your eternal process.

Weaving the Tapestry

Some of the material you will find in this book reflects principles of energy and physics, which I don't go into great detail about here because I feel the coding and decoding process—while intrinsically connected to the science of energy—is the key component. If you would like to learn more about things like *phase entanglement, interconnectedness, adjacent possibilities,* and *consciousness creation* (some of which are briefly mentioned here), I invite you to read my previous books *Quantum Success* and *Secrets of Success.* These books delve much more deeply into the science of energy and consciousness.

In fact, there are so many pieces of the life puzzle that the more I study, the more I realize I have much to learn. And although the basis of this book—the process of the coding technique itself—was not derived through study per se, I have found that there are principles in physics and neuroscience that support this wonderful technique.

The energy system of the human experience is infinitely complex. I have studied the energy of the mind, the chakra system, and the meridians for decades, but I have to thank one person for being a blessing and an unlimited well of guidance, inspiration, and support: Donna Eden, author of *Energy Medicine,* which I highly recommend. Donna has been a pioneer in that field and has developed a system of physical healing that is elegant and comprehensive in its approach. She once taught me an easy method to help with my occasional bronchial issues. It's so easy that I often forget to employ it, but when I finally remember, the breathing problem invariably goes away.

It's funny, but I find the coding technique to have much the same response. It's so easy, people often forget to do it. But please don't make the assumption that it's too simple to be effective—just the opposite is true. So often in life it's the most direct approach that gets the best results!

Some of you may be aware of EFT, Emotional Freedom Techniques, which involves tapping certain points and saying certain statements. While it may sound similar to the coding technique in this book, any resemblance has not been designed by me or directly based in that. I do want to thank Donna's husband, David Feinstein, author of *The Mythic Path* and *The Promise of Energy Psychology* (with Donna Eden and Gary Craig). David introduced me to EFT, and I highly recommend his work as well.

Many practitioners deal with healing reactive patterns. The one who has influenced me the most in this area is Dr. Darren Weissman. In addition to helping me with the physical representations of my own reactive patterns, he has taught me a lot about how they weave themselves into every aspect of our lives. I recommend his work and his books *The Power of Infinite Love & Gratitude* and *Awakening to the Secret Code of Your Mind.*

Interestingly enough, some people have also compared the coding technique to a form of self-hypnosis, and there may be an element of that going on. However, this is much more energetic in nature, involving the neural pathways, balancing brain hemispheres, and helping to initiate alpha-level brain frequency, which is both relaxing and creative at the same time.

It is sublimely interesting that although the process itself is energetically focused on the brain, it leads to a far greater heart-centered approach to life.

A Letter from My Heart to Yours

Any similarities to other techniques are either accidental or perhaps intended by Spirit. In fact, I don't take any credit at all for creating this technique. I'm just the messenger, and I've been asked to tell you about it. From the results I myself have experienced and from what others have shared, there's an important purpose in conveying this information.

All the coding cases written about in this book are true, although I have changed the names to protect people's privacy. Several different types of problem patterns have been totally reversed with the use of this technique, from dealing with addictions like smoking and overeating, to eradicating fears and phobias like fear of public speaking and driving phobias. They have all been so impressive, and I applaud and thank all the people who have shared their experiences and taken the action to make such significant changes in their lives.

It is especially touching to me to see the deep inner changes that people are making. They have been able to build confidence where there was none before; create the genuine happiness that has eluded them their whole lives; heal their own broken, blocked-up hearts; and finally receive real love—both from themselves and others.

This emotional healing is the real breakthrough. It shatters the blocks that many people are facing. They've buried the pain, but they still live with the results. Old feelings of abandonment, fear, rejection, and hostility leave deep codes that can establish a very negative direction. But even with the most difficult of histories, we all have the ability to finally break through and create the life we want.

It is for that reason that—after a few years of testing—I now bring this process to you. I ask you to try it with an open heart and never give up! I am interested in hearing about your results. In order to help out, my website, sandrataylor.com, has a number of free audio downloads on igniting your Quantum Power and Attracting Success. Also join me on Facebook.com/SandraAnneTaylor and on Twitter @SandraATaylor for daily inspiration and insights—and to connect.

Always remember, you are an energetic being in an energetic world, and you have more power than you know. Clear your own blocks, open your energy to the river of abundance that flows all around you, and get ready to jump in!

PART I

DISCOVERING THE REALM OF CODES

*"The primal cause is mind.
Everything must start with an idea.
Every event, every condition,
every thing is first an idea in the mind."*

— **Robert Collier**

CHAPTER 1

THE HIDDEN POWER WITHIN

"Something deeply hidden must be behind things."
— attributed to Albert Einstein

The Universe is awash with energy. In fact, it is *all* energy. From the most dense and solid object to your own beating heart, the vibrations of yourself and all the world around you never stop. Of course, there are lots of different types of energy swirling about—energy that connects us, influences us, leaves us, and returns. Everything pulsates with vibration; and in the natural, healthy state of things, there is a synchronistic Universal flow.

The world we live in is a dazzling river of amazing potential. Sometimes events seem totally random, yet other times it seems there is purpose and direction—a motivating force. In the quantum physical world, the consciousness of humanity creates reality, and the undeniable truth is that your consciousness creates your individual reality as well.

But did you know that there are hidden codes that feed your consciousness? They shape your life with the power of a bulldozer carving out the road in front of you, leading you in the direction that your codes determine. So if you don't like the road you're on, you'll need to look at and change the codes that brought you here.

These powerful inner influences cannot be denied or simply shrugged away. They are written in your unconscious mind, in your daily life, and in your automatic responses to the world. They not only direct the never-ending script within your head but also bring a significant power to bear on the outer direction of your destiny as well.

Even now, without your knowledge, a deep and sustaining code is running through your life. And depending on the nature of its message, it can be the source of wonderful experiences—or it can easily block your desires and ruin your attempts to be happy. You can find the signals of your codes by examining the outward patterns of your life. If you're meeting with repeated frustrations, there's likely something negative encoded.

Yet even the strongest negative code can be broken. New and life-affirming codes can be created, bringing profound happiness and surprising fulfillment of your dreams. This is what happened to a friend of mine named Bob who experienced a complete reversal in his *lack-of-love* life.

The Amazing Story of Bob Decoded

Bob was a wonderful man—smart, sensitive, communicative, and generous to a fault, and on top of all that, he was also handsome and wealthy. He was just the kind of guy most women would be thrilled to be with. The problem was, he didn't attract (and wasn't attracted to) most women. No, he constantly found himself falling in love with very selfish and emotionally unavailable women.

Believe it or not, in spite of everything Bob had going for him, he was a 50-year-old man who had *never* truly been loved. His mother had been demanding and critical, and Bob had spent much of his life bowing to her will, becoming a successful doctor and even building some significant holdings in real estate. No matter how well Bob did, however, he never really received his mother's approval. There was always more that he should do, and her genuine love was constantly being withheld.

When Bob finished med school, he started dating a young woman who would set the mold—and the code—for virtually every romantic relationship to come. This young woman was bright and attractive, but like his mother, she placed a lot of demands on him. And when it came time for him to start his practice, both his mother and his girlfriend told him it was also time that he should get married. So in spite of not feeling a real love for or from this woman, Bob followed the path of least resistance—along with his long-held code of subservience in the pursuit of love and approval.

Bob's marriage was perfunctory. He had three children—all girls—each of whom perpetuated his patterns of being only on the giving end with the women in his life. As time went on, Bob found himself growing in a different direction, wanting to understand the deeper meanings behind things. He engaged in some spiritual study, but above all he longed to break through the emptiness and loneliness that had pervaded his personal life.

Now, Bob was a brilliant man, and as a doctor he understood the connection between mind, body, and spirit in the pursuit of wellness. He continued his medical practice, but he also started to investigate things like meditation and alternative healing techniques. Whenever he attended a class, he always invited his wife to go with him. Her only response was to mock him and make disparaging comments to their daughters.

Bob tried several approaches, including counseling, to remedy the matter, but the situation only grew worse. After a couple of years of feeling ostracized from his own family, he realized that the necessary next step was a divorce.

Eventually Bob started dating again, but time after time he found himself in relationships with women who were selfish, self-serving, and dismissive of him. He was loving and generous, but the women he dated took advantage of that and often used him for his money. And in many of the cases, especially at the beginning, Bob felt compelled to use his money as a way to keep things going. It wasn't surprising then that as his daughters grew up, they took the same approach and would engage with him only when there was something in it for them.

Bob was desperate for love and willing to do pretty much anything to make it happen. Yet he knew on some level that real love was not coming his way. In fact, he always ended up feeling used and dismissed—frustrated or hurt by pretty much every woman in his life.

Over and over again I watched as he fell head over heels for beautiful yet selfish and demanding women. He always hung on, hoping that something would change and a genuine connection would be forged. Unfortunately, the women never truly related to him or even made him a priority. They were physically present but emotionally absent and never interested in his desires or needs.

He was on the outside looking in—looking for approval, but really longing for unconditional love and a genuine heart-to-heart connection. This had been his persistent pattern since childhood, and although it was Bob's deepest desire to change it, it was also his unchallenged code and his subconscious belief that his attempts at love could only end in pain.

The Code's the Thing

Every individual has a DNA code that is unique. This code contains specific information determining things like hair color and eye color, and markers that can indicate anything from the likelihood to be overweight to the possibility of illnesses to come.

Until relatively recently, it was assumed that our DNA code was set for life and could not be altered. Recent scientific evidence, however, shows that even the singularly unique, seemingly stable DNA code of an individual can be changed through the process of epigenetics. That is, through our environment and lifestyle changes, we can change the direction that our physical health may be going. This is a surprising and liberating revelation, and it's not the only code of yours that can be changed.

Like Bob, you have unspoken codes that are hidden within you. They don't take the shape of the double helix of your DNA—in fact, they don't take any physical shape at all. Instead, these codes are written deep within your nature, within your emotions, thoughts, behaviors, and energy. They can motivate you, determine the direction of your life, and even define you *without* your knowledge. Something so powerful deserves to be investigated.

What Lies Beneath?

The word *code* has many definitions, one of which is *a set of rules or standards adhered to by a group or individual.* Would you be surprised to know that you have created (or at least accepted) a set of rules or standards by which you live your life? In fact, these guidelines are woven through almost every aspect of your daily experience. It's true for all of us—even if we have never looked at it quite this way.

Almost everyone forges an entire network of reactions and impulses that govern their choices and behaviors. These codes are often set very early in life—usually by the age of six or seven. Some of them are fairly obvious. For example, if you were taught at a young age never to interrupt when someone was speaking, that will probably be one of the codes you live by. And if you were taught to take your shoes off when you enter a house, that's another. These are both relatively harmless, innocuous rules that probably don't have a lot of influence in your life.

However, if you were taught that you were stupid or inadequate, that could create a debilitating code that could virtually ruin your life. And if you're female and have been taught that women should be marginalized and have very few opportunities in this world, that deep-seated code could severely limit your very approach to life.

These "guidelines" usually come from our parents, our culture, and others around us. Many are coded for generations, potentially becoming a part of our cellular memories and emotional mind-set. And even if they're truly unhealthy and totally unconscious, we all too often willingly embrace them and live in their negative momentum regardless of their consequences.

Fortunately, it doesn't have to be a laborious task to shift the unwanted codes that have been driving you. There's an easy yet powerful technique that you can use in your daily life to shift your codes, your consciousness, and your ability to be happy, breaking through patterns at the quantum level, the deepest vibration of your life-force energy. Those vibrational changes then pave the way to new, fulfilling patterns in work, relationships, and personal pursuits, opening your life to the very real and appealing results that you've been waiting for.

Bob's Coding Cure

Being the investigative, spiritual, and determined man he was, Bob used many techniques to work on changing his relationship patterns. But when he added the specific decoding and coding process described in this book, things really started to shift in leaps and bounds.

In Bob's case, the energetic repercussions of his history were clear. He had developed a deep (yet largely unconscious) code of undeserving mixed with the very real expectation that in any relationship he would only be used. This code filled his consciousness and defined his reality, forging unhappy patterns that dominated his life.

Bob hadn't even realized that he was living with this core code of unworthiness. He longed for a real relationship, but his unconscious conviction (springing from his mother's constant negative input) was that due to his unworthiness, the Universe just couldn't provide a mutually nurturing and loving relationship. And after all his experiences, he felt he was doomed to stay stuck in this pattern forever.

When we investigated his inner codes, here's what we found:

Desperation: Having a life totally lacking in love created a profound and unquenchable need in Bob, an urgency that pushed away the very type of person that he was longing for. This is a function of the energy of Paradoxical Intent, which says that the more desperate you are, the more you push your desire away. Bob's desperation was deeply coded, arising every time he met someone he thought could be "the one." But that urgent code actually repulsed the loving, stable people he longed for, and attracted women who were as needy and urgent as he was—only in their case, they were desperate for material gain.

Bob used the decoding technique to release that desperation, and for the first time since his divorce, he found that he could be truly peaceful and happy on his own. He could now go out with his male friends and have real, present, and relaxed fun. Prior to this, when he went out with the guys, he really was always trolling for women—constantly on the lookout for the next woman who might love him. He was elated by how liberated he felt at being released from that shackle of desperation—finally able to live an enjoyable life that wasn't being filtered through longing and need.

False beliefs of beauty and value: Through his experience, Bob had formed the opinion that all beautiful women were superficial and self-serving, yet he desired a loving relationship with someone he was attracted to. So he decoded the false belief that beauty was just a package for selfish mean-spiritedness. He also coded the ability to see the loveliness of everyone he met, along with the ability to be attracted to a woman's inner beauty—heart and soul.

Undeserving and self-judgment: Bob's code of unworthiness and self-judgment had been written in childhood and willingly embraced ever since. He used the technique you'll learn in Part III to decode those patterns of finding himself faulty, along with any conclusions that he didn't deserve love. He did this repeatedly, determined to write a new story for himself. At the age of 50, he now knew that he had the option to create an entirely new, healthy, and empowered code for himself—and he went about doing it!

Bob coded a genuine deserving of kindness and reciprocity in all his relationships. He also coded the ability to discern real love and the knowledge that he was worthy of a mutually nurturing romance, one where he was valued for himself and prioritized by his partner.

In addition to that, he also coded all of the following:

- The ability to be happy even when not in a relationship
- The ability to find peace in his relationship with himself
- Unconditional self-acceptance
- Genuine self-love

Bob and I did several of these coding sessions, and he soon felt better about himself and his life. Six months after he started this process, he told me that he'd met someone really special. She was interested in the same things he had been pursuing, and she was authentic and kind, a wonderful woman in a beautiful package. He said that he was taking it slowly, not jumping in, not being urgent and desperate like he'd always been before.

That relationship has grown and flourished. His inner codes had shifted and the nature of his relationship experience had completely changed. In fact, he called me to tell me that he had come home from work one day and found his new love cleaning his house and cooking his dinner. While this may not seem like a big deal to many people, Bob told me in a joyful voice that no one had ever done something like that for him—just for him—without wanting something in return.

Bob was finally happy. He had liberated himself from the old code that had kept him stuck in the same old relationship pattern over and over again. He released the assumption that only a relationship could bring him joy, and he coded genuine happiness on his own, harnessing the power within. And that profound shift in his energy opened up a world of new and joyous experiences. Even his daughters were starting to treat him differently!

This is a true story. And if you knew Bob like I do, you'd have found it impossible to believe that someone so wonderful in so many ways could have been so "unlucky" in love for so very long. Well, it wasn't about luck at all. It was about a deeply powerful but hidden code that he had been carrying for his whole life.

Many of us are in a similar position, unknowingly blocked without a clue as to what to do about it. But the Universe created an entirely new response to Bob's new code, and the same can happen for you. No matter what you've been going through, you can shift the old codes that have been keeping you stuck. Freeing yourself from those unhappy patterns is, in itself, valuable and life changing. It brings an energy of happiness and peace that fills your life from day to day. It aligns your life force with all the hidden power and potential that the Universe has to offer.

CHAPTER 2

CORE REACTIONS

*"From science and from the spiritual
experience of millions, we are discovering
our capacity for endless awakenings in a
universe of endless surprises."*

— **Marilyn Ferguson**

There's magic going on within you—an energetic kind. You are pulsating with physical, mental, emotional, electromagnetic, and subtle energies right at this very moment. Your brain alone is a generator of all sorts of energies and experiences in your daily life, producing neurotransmitters and neuropeptides that affect (and are affected by) your emotional state. The energetic implications are significant. In fact, there are more connections in one square inch of your brain than all the stars in the cosmos. And if all the neurons in your brain were to fire at once, it would create enough electricity to light a lightbulb!

The power of your energetic makeup could perhaps be the most important factor in the emotional quality of your life. But it doesn't stop there. The energy of your mind, body, and spirit—in other words, your life-force energy—is viable and powerful. It travels through you and from you in fields of vibration and information, coding, connecting, and communicating with individuals and the world around you. And the consequences of those connections are transmitted back in time and space for you to experience and behold.

Imagine yourself at the center of a huge electrical grid. You're a powerful generator of vibration that moves outward from you, first through the intimate relationships and experiences of your life, then farther outward to acquaintances and even to others you may have never met. Your energy then moves out to the ends of the Universe. It's a flow of light, vitality, and information, projecting to the farthest reaches of the cosmos.

But what happens if there's a power outage, an energy block, right there at the core? The energy gets stuck in the center of your own life-force powerhouse. The connections aren't made, and the world—at least in the affected areas—goes dark.

I remember in 2003, when a single power station in Ohio knocked out the electrical power throughout the northeastern United States and parts of Canada. There was a run on flashlights, batteries, and candles, as the lights were out for several days. When an event like this happens, the people in charge have to go to the source to figure out what stopped the energy and to get things rolling again.

This is a very apt metaphor for the movement of your own personal energy, both within you and projecting outward. It's clear that *you* are at the center of an elaborate network of Universal energy. But *what* is at the center of *your* energy? The answer to that question is important if you want to keep an open, flowing channel to the wonders and beauties of the world around you. But it's even more important if you want to keep the flow of happiness moving within your life.

Energetic You

Your own personal grid is made up of energy centers (also called *chakras*) and complex meridians, a collection of points that help your vital life force move within you in ways that can keep you emotionally and physically healthy. These chakras and meridians are important channels of the personal currents of your mind, body, and spirit. And when these channels are open and healthy, you can use this amazing energy to your advantage—both within your personal life and as strong intentions projected outward into the energetic realm.

There is an elegant system of synchronicity that responds to the clear and fluid movement of your energy. But to really have things align in your favor, you have to keep *your* energy flowing. Your physical health, your emotional balance, your life force, your happiness, and your personal success depend on it.

The fact is, your old traumas, emotions, and beliefs can accumulate in your energy field, lodging in your cellular memory and in your physical and energetic body. This accumulated energy can block the open, flowing current of your life force, creating an imbalance in both body and mind. The result is a personal resonance that could be fragmented, dense, or even completely blocked. And when your inner energy gets stuck, your outer life gets stuck as well.

Blocked energy can manifest in persistent emotional patterns such as chronic depression, high anxiety, or even just dissatisfaction or unrest. The momentum of such negative patterns then results in repeated life difficulties, such as always attracting unavailable partners or continually finding yourself in overstressed and unappreciated job experiences—to name just a few of the common problems your blocked energy could cause. Such negativity becomes a part of the personal code that generates your emotional energy and directs your life. This is what happened to Bob, whom you read about in the last chapter, and his relationship experiences reflected his inner unhappiness.

Code Map

Codes weave themselves through almost every arena of our lives. They are systems of information and influence that shape our physical, emotional, relationship, and even financial destinies. So in order to direct these important influences, it's necessary to investigate all the layers of meaning of this compelling network.

1. Your Personal Code

Everyone has a truly unique code that in many ways describes and defines them. Your DNA is considered a singular genetic code that is yours alone. Within that individual code, however, are many specific codes that identify such physical markers as your hair color, your likelihood to be tall, and the potential for contracting certain diseases, among numerous others.

This is similar to your own personal energetic and emotional code. It's a singularly unique representation of the whole of you. Yet within this all-encompassing personal code are untold specific codes of thought, behavior, emotion, and energy, all of which reveal patterns of the past and potential for the future. These include the reactive patterns that are deeply coded, driving forces in your life. And like the expression of your DNA, with certain genes being "turned on" or "turned off," these energetic patterns can be changed according to the choices and behaviors you engage in on a regular basis.

2. Your Eternal Code

Within your personal code is a part of your identity that existed before this life and will continue long after. This is your soul code, the core of truth and vibration that carries your eternal spiritual identity. This inner code is perfect and peaceful, yet unendingly powerful. When we awaken to this code—which is the central marker of who we are and what we're capable of—it shifts our consciousness from the limited and negative codes of our reactive patterns and opens our life to all the potential the Universe has to offer.

3. Your Quantum Breakthrough Code

Your network of physical and energetic identities can be unlocked and shifted in many ways, especially through the technique you'll learn in Part III, which is itself a code. The process of the Quantum Breakthrough Code lays open the old, unwanted patterns that may haunt you and quite literally rewrites your code in more healthy and empowering ways. Like the binary code that forms the language of a computer, the technique forms a new language of thought and responses for you to live by.

It's important to know that this is not just a series of affirmations with a physical cue. Rather, it's an energy-shifting technique. There are two halves of the breakthrough code. The first is the decoding part of the process. Once you release those reactions that have been driving you in the wrong directions, you're free to move on to the second half of the breakthrough code. This is the part of the technique that unlocks all the wonderful energies and the breakthrough forces that are lying dormant within. It's the key that opens the door to real happiness and fulfillment.

Loaded (Coded) Questions

In addition to all its other meanings, the word *code* implies *hidden information,* a secret message stored within. So to learn more about your inner codes, take a moment to consider these questions. When you have the time, answer them in your coding journal:

- What do you think is the secret information that you carry within and about yourself?

- What are the thoughts you think about yourself—things you may not share with anyone else?

- What are the inner worries that never seem to leave you alone?

- What are the most common emotions that thread throughout your day?

All these items reveal the coded messages hidden within, and many have been your constant companions since childhood. But the most important question you need to ask yourself now is this:

- Do you want to continue living with those old codes and keep perpetuating the unwanted

patterns of your life—or do you want to break
through and create a new code that leads you
in an entirely new direction?

That question is what this book is all about. As you'll
discover, the codes of your subconscious and conscious
mind govern your emotional experiences, your chemical
reactions, and in many ways your external results. If you
don't like what you've been experiencing, if you want to
change the mental and emotional patterns that drive your
life forward, you now have the option to fundamentally
change your codes. You *can* break through the old patterns
that have been keeping you stuck, and replace them with
wonderful new codes of joy, energy, and enthusiasm. And
like the knights of the Round Table, whose code of chivalry
motivated and guided them, your new magnetic codes can
fill your life with present happiness and create undiluted
excitement for all your adventures and achievements yet
to come!

The Patterns of Your Life

The nature of the quantum world is energetic, and
you can be sure that your own life-force projection picks
up a directional momentum according to your ongoing
patterns of consciousness—even if those patterns are all
*un*conscious. You may never consider the consequences of
how you think and live your life, but your consciousness
will continue to create your reality anyway. This is actually
very liberating because when healthy patterns are activated
and unhealthy patterns are released, more powerful personal forces can be engaged. Your life becomes happier
and calmer, and as a result, your consciousness can create
far better results.

The first step in making these changes is to examine what's going on under the surface in the spontaneous, often unconscious, habits called your *reactive patterns*. Many of these are unhealthy and difficult to deal with, but whether you want to examine them or not, it's important to know that they're the major triggers of the negative emotions that could be keeping you stuck. The fact is, you live with your reactive patterns every single day, and this is where your dominant energy and inner codes can be found.

These persistent habits quietly build a strong momentum that directs your life. Although they're often based in your history, they manifest in every part of your present experience, including the behaviors you engage in, your perception of yourself, and your sense of power in the world.

This is an energetic truth for all of us. Our spontaneous reactions to the people and situations in our lives eventually become deeply indoctrinated habits that perpetuate repeated responses and accumulate difficult experiences. For example, an old failure in business can become a self-perpetuating expectation, creating a pervasive mood of depression or even hopelessness where work is concerned. Your unhappiness not only colors your life but also darkens the potential for the career success that you desire.

But you can take a quantum leap to shatter your old negative patterns and ignite the breakthrough forces that will change the quality of your life. It's not just about positive thinking, although that certainly helps. It's an actual energetic process that can help you *break through* your persistent reactive patterns. In time, you'll be able to achieve happiness as your new reactive pattern, and that vibrant and beneficial resonance will lead to the pleasing results you long for.

This isn't just a function of wanting better things, however. It's driven by the desire to free yourself from the codes of lies and limitations that have woven themselves into the fabric of your life. By relieving yourself of the weight of these habitual distortions, you will finally gain the freedom to be your authentic self. Such profound freedom and authenticity will shift the very core of your consciousness, charging your life with enormous amounts of happiness and joyous energy.

How Do You React?

The conscious or unconscious patterns that crank out your emotional and personal reality are most often found in how you react to the people and experiences in your life. So you need to ask yourself, Do I generally react to things with a patient and calm approach? Or do I consistently react in worry, fear, anger, impatience, self-judgment, or other negativity? Write down your thoughts in your coding journal.

If you live in the list of agitated reactive modes, you'll not only perpetuate an undercurrent of unhappiness but also keep getting the same negative results. But you don't have to give up. No matter how consistent any negative pattern is, you can decode the old patterns, defy fear, stop addictions, shift emotional currents, and develop a profoundly peaceful and productive way of living!

The Components of Reactive Patterns

It won't be hard to identify the underlying patterns of your life. In fact, as you go through this book, you'll probably recognize them pretty readily. And just as they won't be difficult to identify, they will also be easier to recode than you may think. So in order to prepare for the greater changes and significant happiness to come, consider the following factors contributing to your hidden (and not-so-hidden) network of reactions.

1. Strong emotions and highly charged events: Most often, our negative habits are sourced in the uncomfortable feelings of difficult or even traumatic events of the past. Of course, positive patterns can be sourced in happy events, but those vibrations do not block the flow of our energy. In fact, they can accelerate the positive codes that enhance our life force.

On the other hand, if you were beaten or emotionally or verbally abused as a child, it's likely that the reactions of fear, rage, and even self-loathing have become deeply encoded and a part of your energetic signature. Even now, if you are around an abrasive, hostile, or even just strong person, you could react in the same uncomfortable ways. Such unhappy emotions inevitably lead to negative and fraudulent conclusions, which are the second component of your driving reactive patterns.

2. False conclusions, beliefs, and intentions: What happens when, at a young age, you become emotionally coded with negative input or treatment from the very people you should be able to trust? What happens with your life force and your personal code? Deep within, you establish a strong belief structure that adds firm but *false* conclusions to the emotional component of your reactive patterns. You are confused and hurt by mistreatment, coding both a deep sense of powerlessness and the assumption that you must be faulty in some way. You *believe* in your powerlessness; you *believe* in your undeserving; you *believe* that you're not valuable. And those beliefs play out in the very manner in which you experience life itself. They become a part of the code that keeps you expecting more of the same.

Now, your past may not have been horrible at all. You may just have been exposed to some skewed parental belief about the world or your power in it. Beliefs like "The world is unsafe," or "Life is hard," or "Only a lucky few get ahead" could now be rattling around in your code and unconsciously directing your destiny.

These patterned reactions may be based in the past, in some kind of mistreatment—or just misinformation—that over time has created an allergy of sorts—one that makes you "break out" in negative thought reactions whenever you're exposed to the same kind of energy, issue, or idea. But when you decode those old beliefs, you can release their influence and carry a new, empowered code, an honest and honoring belief about your value and power—and about the greater potential of the world around you.

Unfortunately, if you're like most people, your *distorted* conclusions actually form the bulk of your consciousness creation—and the direction of your energetic vibration. These beliefs can be deeply layered and multidimensional, which means your inner consciousness can contain gripping codes that go beyond your unhealthy emotions, thoughts, and beliefs, reaching into your chronic behaviors, which form the third component of your reactive patterns.

3. Chronic habits of familiarity and ongoing choices: When we try to cope with the pain from the past—and the self-sabotaging beliefs of the present—we often feel the need to escape. We engage in habits that seem to comfort us at first, but eventually become another layer of reactive pattern. What seems like *coping* is really just *coding* a new addiction or habit of escapism, which only digs us in deeper.

For example, you may drink to escape a core reaction of self-hatred. But over time you find that you need to drink more in order to continue to "feel better." This, however, just causes you to judge and loathe yourself even more. So the initial reactive pattern of self-criticism expands, and the behavioral pattern of drinking is added on. Through this vicious circle, these unconscious reactions can completely drive your destiny in directions that you feel you have no control over.

It's true that some habits die hard, and addictions are especially tough, but as we shall see in the cases discussed in upcoming chapters, the decoding and coding techniques can activate powerful energetic interventions. Smoking and overeating are daily forms of escapism, but even these patterns can be decoded. And through a new code, personal power and real freedom will be achieved!

When we look underneath the surface, it's easy to see how our hidden codes and negative reactive patterns could hinder or even completely block the activation of our true happiness and magnetic energies. But no matter how deep and dark the old resonance is, no matter what it may be concerned with—behaviors, emotions, mental condition, financial state, or even relationships—it can be released and rewritten. And a brand-new reality can take shape and forge a new self-definition.

In the center of your personal code, you carry unlimited power. You can harness that power at any time to create profound illumination and joy. When you strip away the patterns that have been keeping you stuck, you can reach down to the core of truth within. Like a nuclear generator, when this core is activated, your life will shine with a beautifully radiant energy for all to see.

CHAPTER 3

SIGNATURE ENERGIES

"What lies behind us and what lies ahead of us are tiny matters compared to what lies within us."

— Henry Stanley Haskins

Our minds are constantly on the go, spinning out thought after thought, belief after belief, reaction after reaction. The patterns of our neural pathways are so deeply entrenched and so spontaneous that it sometimes seems as though someone else is driving the bus up there!

It doesn't take much to get our patterns of reaction going. For example, if you were bitten by a dog in your youth, it may have caused you to have fear thoughts every time you saw a dog for years after that incident. That neural pathway was forged, and it became your predominant reaction to dogs. Even as an adult, the fear thoughts may be more subconscious and less noticeable, but you could still tense up when this neural pathway is triggered by seeing a dog.

In fact, we are always in the business of creating thought, emotion, and energy. It may sometimes be unclear as to which part of the formula comes first, but it's an absolute truth that thought is always a predominant factor. It's hugely influential in our codes, and that's why it's such a powerful choice to spend some energy on our thought patterns and rewire our neural pathways.

Brain Waves—Business as Usual?

Much of the work I did in my psychological practice was cognitive therapy—teaching people how to retrain their thinking in more positive and optimistic ways to reduce worry and have a greater sense of well-being. I found this to be hugely successful; countless people were able to recover from debilitating phobias and overwhelming depression this way, combined with relaxation techniques.

The benefits of this approach are widely accepted in the psychological community and were corroborated when a university study worked with two groups of highly anxious and worrisome people. One group was given SSRIs (selective serotonin reuptake inhibitors). The other group was given intensive cognitive therapy. After six months, each group showed the same increase in their levels of serotonin, which is the neurotransmitter that enhances one's sense of well-being. Such is the power of thought on your brain chemistry!

The brain is a magnificent machine. In spite of former assumptions, it has recently been proven that through the process of neurogenesis we can grow new brain cells throughout our life—especially in the memory cells of the hippocampus. And just as epigenetics (or lifestyle influences) can change the very code of our DNA, neuroplasticity shows that our brain patterns can change as well.

So why do we continue to go through the same old thoughts and the same old responses, allowing the brain to perpetuate the same old patterns in our life? The fact is, our "business as usual" is deeply encoded—and it's going to stay that way until we do something about it.

I still believe affirmations and cognitive restructuring are powerful tools in this regard, but the quantum breakthrough coding technique adds an important missing element: energy! It's clear to me that the energy used in this process focuses your intention, conducts your mental current, and accelerates transformation. It's such an important element, it warrants further investigation.

Energy Central

There's an ancient study of medicine and energy within the human body that dates back over 3,000 years. It examines your flow of *chi*—or life force—and its influence on your health, vitality, and well-being.

There are seven primary energy centers (or chakras, as you read in Chapter 2) that channel your vital life force. They run through the center of your body from the base of your spine to the top of your head, and each one corresponds to the organs of the body that surround it—and to certain issues in the human experience. When you clear the muck that's keeping you stuck, you open blocked energy centers and ignite the powerful breakthrough forces that will activate the major shifts you're longing for.

The breakthrough coding position utilizes certain centers to channel energy through your mind, change present patterns, and establish new neural pathways. So it's important to know just a little bit about where these centers are and what they do.

In addition to your seven primary energy centers, there are also six secondary chakras, which are at the palms of your hands, the bottoms of your feet, and your ears. The coding technique also employs chakras at the tips of your fingers, which are a part of the 20 tertiary, or third-level, energy centers at your fingers and toes.

This is a highly organized and interconnected system that allows your energy current to move through all your meridians and all your chakras. This flowing *signature* vibration of yours is filled with information, pulsations, and patterns that never stop influencing your physical, mental, and emotional reality. Whether you've been aware of it or not, this ongoing process—whether fluid or blocked—can be a significant source of (and a powerful solution to) many of the issues you face.

Keeping the energy moving is the key, and in the case of the coding technique, the energy gets going when we finally break through our chronic codes of unhealthy thought and response patterns. The habits of negativity keep us on the same old treadmill, grinding out the same old consciousness, and expending a whole lot of energy but never really going anywhere. That's why this technique is focused on the energy center that rules thought, vision, and brain activity—the brow chakra. Let's take an introductory look at the process itself.

Sneak Peek at the Coding Technique

The Quantum Breakthrough Code works on an energetic level to dismantle deeply encrypted unwanted patterns and to establish new resonant vibrations of thought and emotion. For this reason, it is actually two processes rolled into one. Each of them, the decoding and the coding, are explained in much more detail in the upcoming chapters. But in order to understand how it works energetically, I'm going to give you a little sneak peek here. It's like diving into the deep end of a conceptual pool, so take it slowly. It's really not as complicated as it sounds.

The decoding position calls for you to place your fingertips on your forehead near your brow center, resting the first two fingers of *each* hand on *either side* of the energy center known as *the third eye.* This location is explained in more detail in Chapter 8, and there's an image there to help you understand it better. But just to get a sense right now of how the position feels, rest your fingers over your eyebrows near the center of your forehead. The fingertips of one hand should *not* be touching those of the other. This position is designed to channel energy into the brow center through your mind, clearing pathways and funneling out any negative energy.

Once your fingers are in place, close your eyes and, while keeping them closed, raise your eyes slightly as if you're looking at that point between your fingertips. While in this position, you can say some sample decoding statements. Try these simple ones at first, or whatever feels right for you: *I decode fear. I decode self-doubt. I decode worry about the future. I decode any resentment for my life.*

Take a deep breath with each decoding statement, and on the exhale, slowly let it go. When you're done with these statements, release your fingers from your forehead, and relax your eyes to finish the decoding process. You may feel a slight tension in your forehead for a few moments because of the unusual posture of keeping your head level while raising your eyes upward. You may even feel some tingling in your palms, fingertips, or forehead, but all these sensations are temporary.

Pretty simple, right? Well, if you think that's easy, here is the coding technique in a nutshell: Place the first two fingertips of just your right hand squarely on the energy center located at the brow. This time you should actually be touching the center (as opposed to being on either side of it). Again, close your eyes, and keeping them closed, raise them slightly as if you're looking at the point where your fingers are touching your forehead. Holding that position, slowly say these sample statements, or whatever feels right for you: *I code peace. I code freedom. I code trust. I code self-love. I code excitement about my life.* Remember to take slow, deep breaths while reciting your statements calmly and comfortably. Again, you may feel a tingling in your palms, fingertips, or head; and you may feel some strain in the muscle area around your eyes, which should dissipate rather quickly.

The Energetic Purpose in the Process

These techniques may sound far too simple or even illogical upon first inspection, but there are important energetic principles at play. The technicalities of these positions do at least three important things that stimulate and accelerate the process of change:

1. **The energy of decoding and coding creates new neural pathways.** Since the focus is on the sixth energy center, the process works directly with the brain, indoctrinating healthy and optimistic patterns of response. These affirmative statements are also likely to produce more neurotransmitters of well-being. In fact, you can code a deep sense of well-being as part of the process.

2. **Raising your closed eyes automatically puts you into alpha brain frequency level**—and with more practice, even into theta frequency. Ranging under 14 cycles per second, these

levels have been shown to be the most creative and productive states of mind—and the most powerful in programming new thoughts and visualizations.

3. **Your change in mental energy dramatically shifts your consciousness and life-force vibration.** Your new resonance will project an entirely different energy, one that aligns with the Universal flow of synchronicity and attracts increasingly better results. This is your quantum connection.

These are just a few of the wonderful effects of this process. The energetic benefits are truly remarkable, so get ready for some significant changes. To facilitate that, make sure you read through the entire book. It will help you understand the reactive patterns you want to decode. It will also reveal the dynamic breakthrough forces that could be ignited through this process. And with their power you can create the best codes—and the best life—possible.

The Quantum Connection

The world is filled with energetic patterns, constantly vibrating in a never-ending give-and-take. Each of us is a part of this perpetual motion, feeding our own consciousness and energy into the mix. The Universe and the people around us will respond according to the kind of life-force projection we send out.

Some of the patterns that determine the results we attract are the workings of the Universal Laws. These natural principles have been talked about a lot in recent years. Unfortunately, they've been oversimplified in many ways, reducing some complex processes of cause and effect to a single simple statement about attraction.

The truth is, there are many layers to the energetic process, and the Universe will respond much more to your network of reactive patterns than to the wishes and desires in your visualizations. That's why the coding technique is so important. The primary energetic purpose is to break through old misery and achieve genuine and pervasive happiness. The results that follow are based in natural law. Your new code of joy carries you on a current of optimism, trust, and peace—all truly magnetic energies that spark wonderful responses throughout your life. For this reason, it's extremely valuable to take a brief look at *some* of the applicable Universal Laws.

1. The Law of Manifestation

One of the most basic natural laws is concerned with how things come into being. For something to exist, it must exist in thought or consciousness first. When it comes to your own individual experience, it means that your own consciousness creates your own personal reality. That is, the information in the thoughts and beliefs that you generate about yourself and your life will move out in time and space and create more of the same.

This is why understanding your reactive patterns is so important. If you believe that you're a failure, your reality will take that shape. If you are very conscious of what you lack, then lack will only expand in your experience. Such belief patterns can and must be decoded so that a new, healthy, and optimistic consciousness can be formed. And coding this optimistic and self-honoring network of beliefs will prove to be a powerful tool in successful consciousness creation.

2. The Law of Magnetism

This law is about energy and emotional vibration. It reveals that, like our consciousness, our life-force energy is projected out into the Universe. But where our consciousness actually forms our reality, our personal resonance attracts people and situations based on how their vibration matches our own.

This life-force energy is filled with patterns of emotional reaction. In fact, it is your predominant emotional energy that will be matched by the Universe, bringing more of the same types of feelings back to you. Luckily, negative emotions can also be decoded, and positive, empowering emotions can be coded in their place.

These aren't just empty words, and I am reminded of their truth even now. As I was writing this, I had a brief but unsettling conversation with someone that was rather overwhelming. It distracted me from my writing and derailed my happiness, too. After allowing this emotional upheaval to take over for nearly an hour, I realized I could stop this reactive pattern. I decoded conflict, unhappiness, and any attachment to what had happened. I then coded happiness, freedom, and present joy. The results were immediate and amazing. I no longer felt upset, and I was filled with excitement and able to focus on my writing again.

Any time you shift out of negative emotion into a happy or peaceful vibration, it changes the resonance you broadcast to the world. The joyous people and situations that tune in to you will fill your life with increasing harmony and good will.

3. The Laws of Desire and Intent

These laws reveal the power of strength and clarity in your intentions. The clearer and less conflicted your desires are, the greater the likelihood of them coming true. However, if your intentions are filled with desperation, that toxic consciousness and agitated energy will actually push your dreams away. Again, it comes down to consciousness creation and a positive vibration. Desperation is based in an awareness of fear and lack, and the misery it causes perpetuates unhappy emotions and abrasive and resistant vibrations.

There are several factors here that are applicable to the coding process. First, it's important to know when you have become urgent about anything you want. That way you can decode that negative emotion and approach the goal or issue with peaceful self-empowerment. Desperation is itself a reactive pattern, and it will always make you feel fearful and powerless. Next, if you follow that up by coding peaceful presence, self-trust, and determination, your focus will be pure and unconflicted. Finally, your intention to create and code real happiness in your present life will not only make that a reality but also create an irresistible vibration that brings even greater joy to you.

The tremendous power of all these laws is stimulated by the seven breakthrough forces discussed in Part IV, but the energetic influence doesn't stop there. When you ignite these dynamic currents, you balance and align your energy centers, creating an open, flowing channel to the synchronistic flow of the Universe.

This reflects the patterns of quantum mechanics, the nature of waves and particles to influence something at a great distance. Your physical, mental, and emotional vibrations are not only contained within you. They move out to create an infinite number of possibilities in your own life and in the world at large. And your life-force influence is enhanced beyond measure when you engage in the seven breakthrough forces.

Because of their very nature, there are energetic connections throughout the breakthrough forces. For example, the three issues of self-vision, self-expression, and self-love, which are located in the brow, the throat, and the heart centers, are all intrinsically connected. When you work on one, you work on all of them, and the new codes you create in any area expand outward to the vibration of all three.

This is true for most of the coding you do. It's a domino effect that opens new, positive neural pathways and clears other important and powerful energy centers. So don't get too worried about what to focus on first. Play with one issue and then move on to others. Use the statements that really resonate with you and open the flow of personal energy that's already vibrating within. The shift can be so stunning, you may be surprised by the results you get. I know I was!

Coding Back to Happiness

A few years ago when I first became perimenopausal, I started having symptoms that I was very unfamiliar with. I could tolerate the physical things like hot flashes; it was the emotional responses that were most difficult. The mood swings, the irritability, and worst of all, the depression really threw me for a loop! These emotions were not only uncomfortable but seemed to be uncontrollable. Extreme lows accompanied a weird chemical feeling throughout my body that exhausted me and sent me to bed—sometimes sobbing in the fetal position. This was not in my nature, and there was nothing going on in my life to cause such severe depression, so I knew it had to be hormonal. I didn't want to do hormone replacement therapy, and since a friend had some luck with an antidepressant, I thought I'd give that a try. Unfortunately, I had plenty of side effects but no relief whatsoever.

The experience became overwhelming for me. I hadn't been accustomed to much depression through my life, and now it was coming without warning or provocation. Sometimes it would last only a few hours; sometimes it would be a few days, a few weeks, or even a few months. Each episode was accompanied by a weird sense of imbalance in my body, and it was never related to any sad or difficult event in my life.

I knew I had to do something, so I used all the interventions I had already incorporated into my life—only now on a more aggressive basis. Affirmations, deep breathing, exercise, and journaling all seemed to help somewhat, but sometimes the depth of the depression was so extreme, it was almost unbearable.

Finally, it occurred to me to use the decoding and coding techniques. Among other things, I decoded the depression and the chemical imbalance that went with it. I coded balance, happiness, and present joy no matter what was going on in my body.

I noticed a few little changes immediately, but I had to be persistent. The depression would come and go and come back again. So I repeated the technique many times a day—although only a minute or two each time. Eventually, I noticed that I was having fewer and less frequent "episodes." I started feeling happier more of the time, and in most cases when it would flare up, all I had to do was a few brief coding sessions and it would be gone!

My kids noticed the difference, too. Some frequent remarks were, "Why is Mom walking around with her fingers on her head?" and later, "Why is Mom singing and goofing around all the time?" Even my secretary noticed I was laughing a lot more, and when she told me that, I decided to code laughter, too.

I felt liberated from something that had seemed outside of my understanding—and completely beyond my control. But after the coding, I was happy again, and whenever that got derailed, I had a tool to fix it right away. The coding technique worked better than the antidepressant I had tried. I could use it as often as I wanted, and the only side effect was joy!

Free and Clear

That imbalance had been unsettling for me. Before I started using the Quantum Breakthrough Code, I felt my heart center shutting down and tears locking up in my throat. My energy was depleted, and a hopeless feeling crept over me, tying me down. Before applying the coding technique, it was a lot of work just getting the depression to a bearable state. After adding the coding, however, it all changed rapidly, easily, and very powerfully. And I am so grateful!

Bob's energy was also stuck in his heart center, and it seemed destined to stay that way. His experience was based on a lifetime of core unhappiness, and his deep code of longing and self-dismissal only perpetuated more traumas of the heart, gathering more pain and more blocks that he had to break through. But through the decoding and coding, Bob was able to shatter even the darkest part of his sad history. It didn't happen overnight, but it did happen, and he has now created a new code, a new energy of happiness that has shifted into a higher and brighter consciousness creation. His new signature energy flowed out and aligned with the Universe, and that synchronicity brought him the person he'd been longing for all along.

There's no doubt that your own signature energy moves out into the world, but its starting point is always within. Your energy centers are like the circuit breakers in your home. If one or more of your energy centers get blocked with old pain and misinformation, it affects the whole; you become unhappy, and your resonance can become dark and dense, a pool of resistant vibrations that make life difficult—and movement forward even harder. Surprisingly, many people actually learn to live in this state of chronic unhappiness and dissatisfaction, never even realizing that they have an alternative!

But just as it is easy to flip the circuit breakers at home, it's also much easier than you may think to flip the switches of your life. No matter how long you've been stuck, your old patterns can be released, and those old codes can be replaced with healthy new ones. And no matter what you've been through, your pipeline of power can start flowing again. So as you move on to Part II, be ready to open up to the information that will get this process going. When you get your energy moving, the power of your own radiant life force will carry you away!

PART II

THE FOUR BREAKTHROUGH STEPS

*"We must learn to view change as a natural phenomenon—
to anticipate it and to plan for it. The future is ours to channel
in the direction we want to go . . . we must continually ask
ourselves . . . 'How can we make it happen?'"*

— **Lisa Taylor**

CHAPTER 4

WHAT DO YOU LONG TO CHANGE?

"The unexamined life is not worth living."

— Socrates

We all have something that could be better in our lives, and we all have persistent patterns that we want to break through. Ultimately it's our responsibility to make the changes we long for. It's not the outer shifts that will solve our problems; it's the inner peace that's the real solution.

Although there are no magic bullets and no perfect pills, there is a relatively easy process that—if you *do* it and *repeat* it—will make a remarkable difference in your life. In fact, you'll be amazed by how helpful the process is. It will be so emotionally empowering, you'll look forward to using it every single day. So get ready for the incredible changes to come!

This decoding and coding technique has some very important purposes, including rescripting your responses, rewiring the brain, and developing new neural pathways. And although it may not feel like it at first, you will be igniting some significant changes in your emotional reactions, as well as in your cognitive responses. Over time you'll notice yourself feeling happier and more empowered, and when something comes up that could derail that happiness, you will have the tools to stay on track.

We know about the brain's ability to change. Old codes can be eliminated, and new codes and new neural-pathway activity can be established. The process found in the four steps of this section, along with the Quantum Breakthrough Code of the next, will give you the power to make those changes. It may look pretty complicated at first, but don't let that deter you. Once you become accustomed to the process, it is very, *very* easy. It actually takes only a few minutes to do, and it can (and should) be done every day.

This liberating approach really helps clear our blocks and connect us with the consciousness field of joy and possibility. Then by coding the healthy ignitors of the breakthrough forces discussed in Part IV, we activate a viable and practical source for peace and happiness in very real terms. Our own alignment synchronizes with the Universe and gives us the power to change our reality as well.

The steps in this section follow a specific order, but you may need to bounce back and forth from one to the other—and from section to section—as you learn how to do the coding itself. Of course, you'll probably have to repeat the process to deal with all your reactive patterns, but don't panic! You'll be able to address each of them, so don't worry about clearing everything in one fell swoop. You didn't create your reality that way, so let yourself re-create it over time. These are deep patterns that you have the power to alter from within. The noticeable changes in your external life experiences will eventually follow suit.

Seeing the Signals

The first step to creating a whole new life is determining what you want (or need) to change in yourself, and this calls for honest investigation. You need to explore your life-force energy to be sure you're addressing the most important—yet possibly subtle—dishonoring or self-sabotaging blocks. In Part IV, you'll explore in depth the patterns that may be obstructing each of the powerful breakthrough forces, and I'll share detailed coding points for each one. To get started right now, let's look at the predominant signals in your present life that can lead you in the decoding direction that's most beneficial for you. Use your coding journal to take note of your responses to the following review.

1. Habitual Signals

Habitual signals are repeated behaviors that are unhealthy, toxic, or dishonoring to you. And yet they are persistently engaged in, often without any conscious thought on your part. These may be escapist patterns like addictions, distractions, or overindulgence. Or they could also be chronic behavioral habits such as laziness, messiness, or constant procrastination. *In essence, habitual signals are any pattern that may feel out of control or self-sabotaging in some way.* You can decode the emotional causes of those habits (like resistance, fear, or unhappiness), as well as decoding the habit itself.

To help prepare for your first decoding sessions, answer the following questions in your coding journal.

- What are some of the habits that you feel are dishonoring to you?

- Can you identify some of the types of
emotions or thoughts that go along with
these habits? Name them in the decoding
statements you formulate in the next chapter.

2. Emotional Signals

The emotions of our lives are the signs of what is going on under the surface. They are the tips of the experiential iceberg. Happy emotions indicate beneficial events and thoughts of appreciation. But difficult feelings may call for further investigation. For example, when we have sadness, anger, rage, shame, depression, fear, or any strong uncomfortable emotion, it usually indicates an undercurrent of negative thinking about a situation. Certain circumstances or specific people may make us feel fearful or powerless, but we can decode both the feelings and any attachments to those involved.

Answer this emotional investigation in your journal in order to line up the most important emotional patterns you want to decode:

- List any chronic negative emotions you'd like
to eliminate.

- List the situations or people that trigger these
emotions. (This will also help you investigate
the next signal of thought.)

3. Cognitive Signals

Entire networks of thoughts and beliefs roll through your life, seemingly with a will of their own. Excessive worry, constant analysis, comparing yourself to others, fear about the future, negativity about yourself or the world—these are just a few of the cognitive ruts people fall into.

No matter how deeply indoctrinated a thought pattern may be, however, it can still be decoded and replaced with a new, healthy, peaceful, and happy perspective. Almost all the reactive patterns you'll look at closely in Part IV are driven by some dishonoring thought or catastrophic assumption.

Use your coding journal to respond to these prompts:

- Examine your beliefs for potential change— what do you *think* about yourself, the people you meet, and the circumstances you're in?

- List any negative or disruptive thought patterns you want to release and decode. Include any negative thoughts about yourself, your future, or the world around you.

Don't get upset if it seems like there are a lot of them. You don't have to decode them all at once—just start with the issues that are most important to you. Most are connected in some way, and as you work on decoding one, you will find the others breaking through as well. Give it time, and let yourself be comfortable in the process. Slowly you'll feel your new cognitions taking shape.

4. Toxic Attachments

Toxic attachments are often found in relationships that are dishonoring or disempowering to you. You may have left someone toxic in the past, but you could still be holding the energy and the conclusions that came from that experience. For example, if someone was dismissive, you may have concluded that you deserve to be dismissed. You may have even gotten into the habit of disregarding and negating yourself.

Another example of toxic attachment is longing for an old, ended relationship. You may still be holding on, even if you haven't seen the person in quite a while, and your emotional attachment shuts down your potential for new love. Or you could still be involved with someone who stimulates a poisonous pattern of reaction in you, such as people pleasing or shutting down and being submissive around that person.

Toxic attachments can also include substances, habits, beliefs, and emotions. We unknowingly become bonded to even our most unhealthy patterns. Things like worry, fear, or perfectionism can actually become addictive—a fundamental part of how we see and define ourselves. Habitual signals, like smoking or watching too much TV, can also become toxic attachments that are hard to break.

Take some time to consider your attachments in your coding journal.

- List any toxic people you want to detach from, along with the difficult sensations or emotions they bring. This connection is important because while a relationship itself can't be decoded, the attachment and toxic patterns that go along with it can be. (For example, when you write your decoding statement regarding this issue, you might say, *I decode any old longing for Jim*, or *I decode fear of Dad*, or *I decode thoughts of unworthiness when I'm around Mom*.)

- List any other patterned attachments to things and attitudes you'd like to decode, including substances, negative ways you identify yourself, or anything you feel you can't control.

5. External Signals

A deeper understanding of your patterns can be gained by examining the outer signals of your life. For example, if you have a life of constant poverty or if you never seem to find the love you want, this could indicate internal issues, such as a poverty consciousness, or perhaps a self-loathing that permeates your energy field. But if you do see these signs in your external world, do *not* fault yourself. Just look for any underpinning negative thoughts, and consider how you can create a loving and productive approach. Decode the fear of poverty or even the attachment to it. (Yes, you *can* be attached to something—or someone—you don't want.) Decode any negative interpretations of yourself or the situation. In every area, code a *successful* self-perception. Also code a sense of safety with money or love, or anything you long for that seems to be blocked. This will change your internal sources so that you can change your external reality.

Use your coding journal to investigate these topics:

- What external patterns do you want to change? Examine work, home, relationships, and hobbies.

- List the emotions or conclusions that go along with each difficult situation.

While you may not be able to decode the external circumstance itself, you can decode the long-held expectation of it. You can also decode any desperation for love or money—or anything else. Take your time. As you shift these codes, you will find an inner peace that's not attached to externals, but that will still help your outer situations shift.

The Methodical Way Out of the Madness

All of this may seem a little daunting at first, but it's certainly worth your time and effort. I did it myself and made a list of all I wanted to recode. Then I started with the issues that were most important to me. As time went on, however, I would randomly pick items to work on—or just do the technique in response to the issues that came up for me.

Let yourself approach this in the way that's best for you. Your preparation, as outlined in this chapter, is an important part of the process. Even if you just jot down a few items, you can go forward with the next steps related to the issues you picked, and you'll lay the groundwork for moving even deeper when you engage in the decoding and coding techniques.

This is the approach that was taken by a client named Claira. She had two major issues she wanted to work on. She couldn't stop thinking about and yearning for a long-gone relationship. She was depressed and overeating, and her other issue was weight loss. She tried to decode her patterns of overeating, but just couldn't seem to break through. So she worked on the sad relationship history instead. She decoded the old attachment to the man whom she thought she still loved, along with the belief that she had to have a relationship in order to be happy. Instead, she coded freedom and self-love—and the ability to be happy right now.

Over time she found herself not thinking about him so much, not wondering what he was doing, not longing for his presence. She found that she was actually able to feel more happiness more of the time. She became more self-directed and more social, too. Eventually she forgot about the man completely.

She's still working on coding the weight loss, but she has found that her old patterns of binging have greatly decreased since ridding herself of that other attachment. Now she's just happy to be happy, and she knows she can break through the rest.

Let yourself start easy. Pick a few important issues and then see what resonates with you most. Like Claira, you're likely to find one issue relating to another. Love yourself through your process. In fact, you can actually code an easy and successful practice of coding. Add joy to the mix, and your life will be a feast.

CHAPTER 5

GETTING READY TO DECODE

"All things are ready, if our mind be so."

— **William Shakespeare**

The next step in this integrative process is to *write your decoding intentions.* These are specific statements designed to be used with the position described in Chapter 8. Consider your impressions from the previous chapters, and use them to prioritize the issues you truly want to change. Determine which ones are more immediate or emotional in nature.

For instance, I had a client who had a fear of public speaking, but had avoided dealing with it her entire life. She found out, however, that she would soon be facing a situation at work that would require that. Although this wasn't the most emotionally charged pattern that she wanted to change, it was the most immediate. So she made that a priority for several weeks. When the speaking event came up, she had successfully decoded her fear and coded genuine comfort instead. The meeting went off without a hitch, and she was then able to move on to some of the more emotional issues in her life.

These are the basics of the decoding intentions—naming the emotions, thoughts, or patterns that you want to rid yourself of. I recommend using the notes you've taken in your coding journal and applying the following process to begin forming your own tailor-made *decoding statements.*

The Language of Decoding

1. Start with complete, specific statements about what you want to decode. These first statements encourage a strong singular intention, specifying the pattern you want to break through in detail.

2. Next, narrow it down and become less specific, but more emotionally focused.

3. Include some statements that decode related issues.

4. Then break down your statements into shorter, more powerful, and more global words and phrases. This creates a more rapid and spontaneous repetition, releasing the old code.

Emma's Old Mind-set

Let's look at some of the decoding statements created by Emma, a client who wanted to lose some weight. She had a very difficult time, especially with the pattern of eating late at night. So her first two statements addressed that specifically:

> *I decode toxic habits of eating late at night.*
> *I decode powerlessness over food—especially at night.*

Then, because she ate a lot in front of the television, she added another sentence.

> *I decode toxic patterns of eating too much while watching TV.*

She then narrowed her statements to the basic issue.

> *I decode any toxic attachment to food.*
> *I decode emotional hunger and unconscious eating.*

And realizing this was an escapist pattern, she also wanted to decode that, adding the following:

> *I decode patterns of escaping.*
> *I decode any fear or loneliness that makes me want to escape.*
> *I decode any need to escape.*

Her ending statements were rapid-fire intentions.

> *I decode unthinking choices.*
> *I decode powerlessness.*
> *I decode loneliness.*
> *I decode longing.*
> *I decode need.*
> *I release it all.*

This is just the first part of the process. All these decoding statements will be followed up with the positive coding intentions designed to reverse the energy. So don't be concerned that this sounds too negative. Remember the quantum connection. If you're living with these negative patterns, their difficult energy is already forging your destiny. The decoding technique is a dramatic approach to releasing the old patterns, paving the way to integrating the new ones through the coding part of the process.

Tips for Decoding

Looking at this example, you may think that you won't know exactly how to write your decoding statements. But don't worry. It doesn't have to be perfect. So many issues are connected, so as you decode one, you decode another. You don't have to know exactly what you want to do or how to phrase it. As you play with this a little, it will become clearer and easier.

Here are some tips that can help you with this part of the process:

- Use your intuition. The right words will come, and deep down you'll know exactly what you want to change.

- Let yourself relax. The statements don't have to be perfect. You can change them up as you continue to use them.

- You don't have to write statements for every issue you want to decode. Pick just a few of your most important challenges. You can always add more later.

- Start each statement with the words *I decode . . .* Begin with longer statements that cover the details. Then narrow in on the predominant thought, emotion, or pattern. You can also start with the words *I release . . .*

- Organize your decoding statements in groups of four to six items relating to each issue. You'll find that some will be repeated, although they may be dealing with different topics. (For example, you may find phrases like *I decode fear* apply to many topics.)

Don't be overwhelmed. Let it be okay to take your time and practice forming the decoding statements that feel right for you. It's not a huge process, but it's an important one. Your willingness to work on this step is inestimably valuable in this life-changing technique. Once you set these steps in energetic motion, you will be amazed by the difference they produce throughout your life.

Peggy's Unhappy Point of View

Let's look at another sample of decoding—this time concerning the more personal and emotional issue of a very negative self-view. Remember Peggy? She constantly scrutinized herself about everything, including her social skills and capabilities at work, comparing herself to others and *always* finding herself faulty in some way. She felt she fell short—with family members, neighbors, and colleagues, always feeling inadequate in their eyes and in her own. As a result, she often worried about what others thought of her and assumed the worst. While many people have this problem to some degree, Peggy's was constant and extreme.

Here are the decoding statements she came up with to deal with this issue:

I decode any old pattern of worrying about what people think.
I decode the habit of worrying about others' judgment.
I decode patterns of self-scrutiny and finding myself faulty.
I decode any patterns of self-criticism and self-doubt.
I decode self-judgment.
I decode self-dismissal.
I decode fear (of judgment).
I decode doubt.
I release it all.

Peggy followed up these statements with her new coding intentions, which you will find in the next chapter. With consistent use, she found that she was more and more comfortable around others, less concerned about what they thought, and increasingly relaxed with family members, friends, and colleagues.

Self-acceptance is a core issue for both happiness and success. So if you find yourself having even fleeting concerns about this issue, use some of the decoding statements above. Follow them up with some of Peggy's new coding statements, and use the technique whenever you feel pulled in that negative direction. You'll feel stronger and stronger, and your life experiences will be filled with a deeper sense of peace.

Determine to Decode

The tapestry we have woven throughout our lives has become the fabric through which we filter all our experiences. But the decoding process helps us change the unhappy pictures and the patterns woven all around us.

If there are dark images threaded through our thoughts and feelings, we can pull those threads and dismantle those codes. It is up to us, however, to determine what we want the tapestry of our life to really look like.

So take the time you need to assemble the decoding statements you want to start with. Just make a few sets at first. You can change them up, rewrite them, or totally switch to another issue if you like. *The important thing is that you actually do this.* Even if you just use the samples given throughout this book, choose the items that resonate with you most. And don't forget to use your intuition—there are always answers there!

CHAPTER 6

CREATING YOUR NEW CODES

*"If we did all the things we are capable of,
we would literally astound ourselves."*

— **attributed to Thomas A. Edison**

The next step to prepare for the coding process is to *create the follow-up statements that respond to the decoding phrases* that were formed in the last chapter. These related codes represent the healthy patterns that reverse the negativity of the issues you wrote about in your decoding statements. You can rewire your reactions to any specific issue, habit, thought, or emotion and provide an empowered and honoring alternative that will become true for you. It may not seem so at the beginning, but in time it will become more spontaneous. Using this positive coding technique will become your natural and predominant response.

Start by writing down longer specific coding statements along with shorter coding intentions that will shift your moods, direct new neural pathways, and change your personal energy. And if you allow yourself to really integrate this into your lifestyle, the coding will establish a resonant, joyful, and magnetic vibration. This technique is the key that will unlock your quantum power to change your energy and choose happiness on a regular basis.

Steps for Creating Powerful Coding Statements

1. Look at the wording of the decoding statements you're planning to reverse, and phrase the new coding statements accordingly.

2. Be specific in your beginning statements; then make them a little more expansive.

3. Shorten the statements even more, focusing on the emotions you want to code.

4. At the end, just use single-word directives, stating the emotion or intention by itself.

Emma's New Code

Let's look at responsive codes to the first decoding sample in the last chapter. Remember, this is just a sample, and you can apply this kind of outline to any issue. Emma's intention was to get rid of her habit of overeating at night and to code new, healthy eating habits anytime. So she responded to her decoding statements this way:

I code healthy habits of eating in control.
I code complete power over food, whether at night
    or in front of the TV.

I code a healthy relationship to food.
I code strength and power over food.
I code power over hunger.
I code feelings of satisfaction.
I code freedom and peace in my heart.
I code healthy, conscious habits.

Then code emotions and states of being that apply to the nature of the issue:

I code freedom.
I am free.

Freedom is an important energy to code and applies to all sorts of issues, including toxic relationships, addictive habits, escapism, longing, fear, and attachment of any kind. All these patterns make us feel stuck and tied up, so it's important to remember freedom as a valuable piece of the coding puzzle. In fact, I use *freedom, power,* and *peace* in a lot of my coding because they're applicable to so many things. Many of your new codes will be greatly enhanced when these statements are added in the coding position:

I code power. I am powerful.
I code strength. I am strong.

And since the final step is to take it down to single-word codes, try holding the coding position described in the next section and simply say:

Satisfaction.
Freedom.
Power.
Peace.

This is an extremely powerful part of the practice. First become accustomed to your longer decoding and coding scripts. Eventually, though, all you'll have to do is quickly engage in the pose and bring in these single words, and you'll feel a shift in your consciousness in just moments. It is truly that powerful! And when you bring your new codes into alignment—from the specific, to the general, to the very powerful single word—over time it will change your experience of life, as it did for Emma.

Emma had lost some weight, but she had hit a plateau that she wanted to break through. She used these coding statements—along with some exercise coding statements we'll discuss later—and she was able to lose another 20 pounds!

Tips for Creating Powerful Codes

This doesn't have to be a complicated process. Make it effective and also easy on yourself by following these tips:

- Phrase your new coding statements in ways that will reverse the energy and the patterns of the decoding statements that you've prepared.

- Again, use your intuition. This should be a heart-centered activity, so don't overthink it.

- Choose strong declarations that start with *I code* . . . or *I am coding* . . . Then narrow it down to specific phrases and individual words. (As time goes on, you'll notice that you can do some coding without the decoding, but the deep issues must be decoded first and followed up with your new specific codes.)

- Don't panic about doing it right—or about doing it at all. It's so easy when you get the hang of it, so don't let yourself be deterred if you find the process a bit daunting at first. Let yourself play with it.

- Try different words until you find the codes that lift your energy the most. When you really start to integrate this, it will be easy to know what to focus on and how to word it— and you'll find it makes a significant difference in your life.

A New Code of Pride

Let's look at another set of coding statements. These were created by Peggy, whose decoding samples were also in the last chapter. She'd been working on changing persistent patterns of chronic self-judgment and self-criticism, all deep codes she had been burdened with since childhood. Here are the new coding statements she came up with to respond to the decoding in the last chapter:

I code comfort and equality around others.
I code self-love and self-acceptance, no matter who's around.
I code honoring self-talk all the time.
I code deep breathing, relaxation, and peace.
I code confidence and a loving self-view.
I code freedom from worry.
I code acceptance.
I code comfort and confidence.
I code self-love and self-trust.
I code freedom. I am free.

Freedom.
Peace.
Love.

Peggy continued using these statements while doing the coding position in Chapter 9, and she found herself accepting their truth. Although she occasionally slipped into wondering about what others thought, it didn't drive her—or upset her—like it had before. Every time the feelings came up, she followed the coding process and reclaimed her self-loving truth. She felt more peaceful around others and was able to engage with her senior colleagues without her former feelings of inadequacy. She even got a big promotion that recognized her talents and capabilities. Now that's a code change—and a quantum breakthrough!

Coding Consciousness

Designing your coding statements can be a lot of fun! Think about all the things you want to create—the states of mind, emotions, and healthy new habits you long to experience. You can code anything you desire, any time you want.

When I'm tired, I code energy. When I feel bored or see the day ahead as a chore, I code excitement and enjoyment. When I find myself going down some negative path, I code trust and peace and the ability to let go. There's always an option to do something different, an *adjacent possibility* to create a new code of reaction, and it's an adventure to see where that new direction leads.

Personally, your own potential is unlimited and expanding, and each and every present moment brings an opportunity for you to reinvent yourself. Even tiny changes can lead to huge transformations in the evolution of your life. This is a function of the complexity theory, where each new adjacent possibility of change can take you to amazing new results.

So give yourself some time to make these little but important changes. Practice the coding and decoding techniques, and jot down your responses in your journal. You'll see that you will tend to use more coding than decoding statements. Decoding is designed to shift old responses, while coding establishes new ones. These statements should be varied, optimistic, emotionally uplifting, and repeated often.

You can use the samples that you find throughout the book, or you can use your own intuition. In fact, at any moment you can ask yourself: *What do I need to feel or focus on now? What emotion or consciousness state do I want to create?* Take a deep breath and code it. As you do so, your sense of self-empowerment will grow and grow.

CHAPTER 7

SETTING THE STRATEGY

"Man is a thought-adventurer."

— **D. H. Lawrence**

You've already done a lot to prepare for the coding technique coming up, and you're probably anxious to get going. In Part III, you'll find out exactly how to do the process itself, but there are just a few more things to consider first. In addition to figuring out what you want to code, you also need to figure out when.

Once you've learned how to do the coding positions, or postures, you'll need to consider the times and situations when you will be using the process. At the beginning, you will want to plan regular times throughout your day when you take a few minutes to decode and code the specific patterns you want to focus on. Schedule the times that are best for you. Since the technique takes only a few minutes, you can fit it in pretty much anywhere. Use your coding journal to note what works and to record ideas about how to fine-tune your routines.

You may have a number of patterns you want to change, so plan to start with your top priorities. Although you don't have to stay with just one, it's good at the beginning to start with one issue for a period of time before moving on to another. You can choose to decode and code one or two challenges for a day, a week, or even a month. Of course, you'll also find that several of your issues are closely related, and your new coding statements will address many of them at the same time.

The Coding Connection

This is exactly what happened to Peggy, the young woman whose statements were displayed in the previous two chapters. It's clear that she had many connected patterns based on her history, living most of her life in judgment and shame, growing up in a large family with parents and siblings who had criticized her and compared her to others. Any acceptance that came her way was conditional—depending on getting the best grades, looking the best, and performing at the highest level. Anything short of the best was never good enough. And even when she did achieve this extreme demand, she always felt as though she had to keep on striving and worrying. She embraced all of this as her own network of reactive patterns, living in self-scrutiny, always judging herself, and constantly esteeming others more highly. She even told me once that she didn't think she'd ever truly been happy—and maybe she didn't even know how.

Peggy had a lot to work on, so she started by decoding self-judgment and coding self-acceptance instead. After several weeks of that, however, she switched to decoding her patterns of striving and comparing herself to others, and then she added personal peace to the self-acceptance code she already had in play. Later, she also specifically decoded the habit of criticizing her looks and added the specific code of seeing herself as beautiful, capable, and happy. As the feelings of well-being grew, she realized that she had indeed created a new code.

It may seem like a lot, but as you can see, all these patterns are connected and are based in the central issue of self-esteem. Although Peggy's decoding jumped from one specific pattern to another, they all eventually lead to a profound new code of heightened self-esteem and self-love. As often happens, similar issues push each other down in a domino effect of changing thoughts and emotions. The results lead to a new core of genuine happiness and self-love—with increasingly joyous results inside and out. Peggy's case was deeply layered and reached down to her core. She went from a nagging fear of being fired to receiving awards and recognition at work. But far more important than that, she went from chronic self-doubt and never feeling happy to finally being at peace in her own skin—and always having the ability to bring her joy back. The quantum changes shifted her energy from deep within, and the Universe responded by opening new doors for her.

Telling Time

Even if your issues are deeply layered and extremely varied, you can juggle them around and deal with them bit by bit. This process is so easy, you can orchestrate it any way you want—but it still has to be done. Whatever you choose to focus on, it's important to set regular time aside. I have found that the optimal times are in the morning and evening. When you first wake up, stop and take a few minutes to decode whatever you're working on, and then immediately code the opposite empowering response. It's also valuable to take a little two-minute break to do the process a few times during the day. Then before bed do the same thing. Those are great times to schedule your process, but you can make it a priority anytime you have an opportunity.

It's also important to consider which situations would be enhanced by engaging in the technique immediately. So ask yourself: *How and when can I activate my new code? How can I shift what's going on in order to enhance my life?* This is a very important piece of the process. There are times when you will want to intervene on old patterns and change the difficulty right in the moment you're experiencing it.

For example, I had a client who had some significant social anxiety. Whenever she was around people—even in small groups—she would get agitated and have a difficult time speaking. It was performance anxiety, really, and it affected her functioning to a great degree. She planned her regular decoding and coding sessions (only about two minutes each) about three times a day—in the morning, at lunch, and during her evening meditation. In addition to that, she planned on doing even shorter, spontaneous sessions whenever she found herself facing any social situation that could trigger her old, very uncomfortable response. As time went on, she found herself getting more and more comfortable with others, so much so that she totally forgot to intervene before the social exposure—yet she felt completely at ease anyway.

So whatever you may be dealing with, right at the time you're feeling the worry, attachment, depression, or fear, take a moment to stop and decode the old pattern. Follow it up by coding trust, strength, happiness, freedom, peace, and any other code that applies to your specific issue.

To figure out the best times for your own *on-the-spot coding interventions,* answer the following questions in your coding journal:

- In what situations do you need help, strength, or just a different emotion, such as happiness, peace, or personal power?

- What habits or emotional, behavioral, or relationship patterns do you want to intervene on?

- When and how can you change those energy patterns?

- What present toxic attachments do you need to shift? What people or situations do you need to re-empower yourself around?

You'll also need to consciously support your new codes in your daily life. Uphold your intentions with your behaviors and choices. For example, if you're working on weight loss, in addition to coding power over food, you can also code the intention to have a drink of water instead of eating. Choose to engage in some other healthy behaviors, and also do some related affirmations. Recognize your power to turn your life around and know that each new choice is actually changing your lifestyle and your energy.

Remember, this powerful process takes only a few minutes to do. But like exercising and eating healthfully, it needs to be done every day if you want consistent and beneficial results. Prepare by having your decoding and coding statements ready—perhaps written on index cards or in a little notebook you carry with you. Then make a specific plan about when you want to do the regular practicing. As you go through your day, notice the appropriate times when you'd like to start inserting the coding process into your routine activities. This provides on-the-spot switching of reactions and emotions. It's an empowering feeling, so let yourself become aware of when you need that shift to occur. These are the trigger points that would usually lead you down the same old reactive paths. But when you consistently reroute them through the coding technique, you will be able to take those moments—and your life—in an entirely new direction.

Emma's Immediate Coding

Emma found it very helpful to do this spontaneous coding whenever her patterns popped up while she was working on losing weight. Of course, she did the regular decoding in the morning, around noon before lunch, and in the early evening so that she would not overeat at night. She followed each one of those decodings with a code of strength, discipline, freedom, and power over food.

After a while, she found that as she was walking to the refrigerator to have one of her late-night snacks of ice cream, she would stop and realize that this was a point where she wanted to intervene. So she would take a moment to decode her hunger, *especially focusing on the deep breathing part of the process.* She followed that with coding statements of inner strength and power over food. But sometimes all she needed was the coding part of the process to break free.

There were occasions, however, when she felt strongly compelled to eat, so she added, *I decode any need to eat. I decode any urgency or need to escape.* Then she coded the willingness to change the habit in the moment, using statements like: *I am powerful. I am peaceful. I have all that I need. I am all that I need.* This helped her to intervene when she was most driven to react in the old ways.

Of course, there were plenty of times when her old behaviors compelled her to give in. In those cases, she coded self-forgiveness and renewed determination. But over time she found that she could simply do a quick coding posture and then find herself walking away from the food and the longing.

You can create a similarly expansive approach to any issue you're dealing with. Plan to do the decoding and coding at regular times—and also at the points you want to intervene. Eventually, like Emma, you may find that all you need is the simple coding technique to achieve your result. Don't limit the activity to just the coding too soon, however. Most of us have lots of reactive patterns to decode, and it is always helpful to remember our intentions to release and let go.

Code Around the Clock

Here are some tips for planning your decoding and coding process times:

- Choose the issues you want to start with, and have your decoding and coding statements ready. You can always change them as you go along. Practice the postures described in Part III using those statements.

- Schedule the times that are best for you to spend just two or three minutes doing the full process. It may take a little longer at the beginning, while you're learning it, but you shouldn't need more than three or four minutes even at that time.

- Write your planned coding times in your calendar, and leave a note for yourself in a conspicuous place to help you remember. Even after doing it for a while, you still have to make the regular practice times an important routine.

- Keep your coding journal and jot down some ideas about when you'd like to intervene on a specific negative pattern during the time it's going on. For example, if you're decoding fear of the dark, you can schedule that— along with the coding alternative of peace and safety before turning out the lights. Or if you're shy and afraid of asking someone out on a date, you can do your process before a party or social gathering. All these intervention codes need to be done *in addition* to the regular practice times.

You're now ready for the special decoding and coding process described in the next section, which are the two components of your Quantum Breakthrough Code. Real change starts with an honest and conscious awareness of the patterns that have been blocking your happiness and keeping you stuck. But whatever those patterns are, you *can* decode them and finally break free. Devote yourself to *yourself!* A peaceful, fulfilling, and happy life is waiting for you. Use the code to go to that wonderful place—and claim it as your own.

PART III

THE QUANTUM BREAKTHROUGH CODE

"It is never too late to be what you might have been."

— **Anonymous**

CHAPTER 8

TIME TO DECODE

*"Whatever you can do or dream you can, begin it;
boldness has genius, power, and magic in it."*

— attributed to J. W. von Goethe

Your mind is like a garden. And when a garden is overgrown with a jumble of uncut weeds, it becomes impossible to plant the seeds of beautiful flowers. Similarly, it would be very difficult to create a garden of wonderful thoughts and attractive energy based on old, unchallenged reactive patterns and negative vibrations. So to establish the happiness and magnetic patterns you desire, it will be vitally important to decode the unwanted "weeds" of reaction that have taken root and spread throughout your life.

There's a freedom that comes from releasing the old, uncomfortable patterns that have consistently blocked your peace and joy. It's a shift that breaks through attachment and clears the way to a depth of inner peace that is rare in this world. Because you will be unraveling the negative codes that have kept you stuck, you may find the decoding process to seem foreign at first. The reason for this is the attachment factor. After all, if you've been living in fear, self-criticism, or hopelessness, you will tend to identify yourself according to these pervasive emotional patterns. And some part of you may actually long to maintain that identity simply because it's all you know!

At first glance, the decoding process may look more complicated than it is. Don't let yourself worry too much about the details. Remember, the quantum connection is all about the energy, and desperate energy blocks the process. So it's important to practice the decoding and coding techniques together *without desperation or concern.* Eventually you'll get the hang of it, and it will become an easy part of your life.

Both the coding and decoding exercises engage the energy center of the mind where a lot of old, reactive patterns can be locked in your mental resonance. Although many patterns are charged with highly emotional energy, the matrix of resonance, emotion, and thought is here at the vibrant energy center of the brain. For example, if feelings of fear and anxiety are predominant emotions for you, they can be traced back to your thoughts about your own powerlessness and worries about the future. You can decode these feelings as well as the thoughts behind them by redirecting the current that moves through this powerful energy center. That's what the decoding process is all about.

The Decoding Position

If you look at Figure 1, at right, you'll find a simple little drawing demonstrating the decoding position. Although it's relatively easy, it's important to know exactly how this posture works. The position starts by touching the first two fingers of each hand to your forehead just to the right and left of your sixth chakra, which is located directly above and between your eyebrows. This is your brow chakra, the energy center most tied in to your mental energy and reactive patterns. There are also energy centers in the tips of your fingers, so when you place the index and second finger of each hand on your forehead around this chakra, it creates an important vibrational connection.

Do not be too concerned, however, about the exact placement of your fingers. The important thing is that the fingertips of one hand should not touch those of the other. This keeps your brow center open, with your right and left hand on either side of it. Then the energy centers at the tips of your fingers can direct the creation of new neural pathways based on your spoken intentions.

This process is designed to run energy from the fingertips of your right hand, opening the sixth chakra into your mind, and then clearing and decoding the unwanted energy patterns out of the left. The left represents the past, both energetically and metaphorically. So it can help on both those levels to end the process by visualizing the cloud of the decoded pattern moving out through the left side of your head or through your left hand, floating out into the ethers—far off into the distance—where it becomes neutral energy. This may sound strange, but it's a powerful technique. By doing this, you're initiating an energetic intention; sparking this powerful chakra; clearing old, stuck energy; and activating the new neural pathways. And all this initiates the quantum breakthrough you're looking for.

Here are some tips that will help you engage in the decoding placement with the greatest comfort and ease—and with the most beneficial results:

- You may find the position easier to do if you rest your second finger along the top of your eyebrows and your first finger against that, placing your fingertips on your forehead as indicated in Figure 1. Some people even rest their thumbs on the sides of the head to anchor their hands in place.

- I have worked with many people who wear glasses, and some have found it easier to take off their glasses first. This may not be necessary, though, especially once you become familiar with the position.

- This may be an unusual position to hold, and although it takes only a minute or two, your arms may get tired at first. Over time, however, you will become comfortable with it. Some people actually do this seated at a table, putting their elbows on the table and resting their heads into the position. With their fingers over their brows and their thumbs anchoring their temples, they are literally cradling their head as they do the process. (Some people have even used this approach at their desks at work.)

- Don't worry about whether you're in exactly the right place. Let your intuition be your guide, and rest your fingertips on either side of that special place called the "third eye." You will sense what feels right for you.

- Some people are concerned about remembering their planned decoding statements while holding this posture with their eyes closed. Make sure you read the statements ahead of time, or if necessary, open your eyes for a moment to review them. You can also make an audio recording and repeat them to yourself as you do the process.

This little position may seem complicated, but trust me when I tell you, it only *seems* that way. Before long, you'll be doing it every day without even thinking about it. As you become more familiar with the decoding and coding process, let yourself approach it in whatever way you feel is most comfortable for you. For example, I have a friend who has a pretty stressful job, and she uses this position to decode stress each day before she goes to work. Then throughout the day, she uses tidbit coding (which you'll learn later in the book) to bring peace and happiness. She finds this an extremely effective approach that has completely shifted her attitude toward work.

The Energy Decoding Process

When you're ready to engage in the decoding position, it's time to do the five steps of the decoding process, releasing the reactive patterns that have been holding you back. This sets the stage for coding new, healthy, and powerful patterns that will bring both personal happiness and joyful experiences. These five steps are neither complicated nor time-consuming. *In fact, the entire decoding process should take only a few minutes.*

Step 1: Place your fingers in the decoding position, take a deep breath, and close your eyes.
Taking the position with closed eyes and a deep breath is just the beginning of the first step. The next part of this step may seem weird, but it is an absolutely important—even indispensable—part of the process.

Keeping your eyes closed, raise them slightly, as if you were looking up at the point between your fingertips. Don't make this stressful or overexaggerated. Simply close your eyes and *gently* raise them up to gaze inwardly at that point between your fingertips.

Step 2: Say your decoding statements while engaged in this position.

Continue to hold this posture, looking upward with your eyes closed, and take a deep breath while saying your decoding statements. You can start with longer statements:

I decode worry about what others think.
I decode the pattern of fearing the future.

Then go to something more basic:

I decode worry.
I decode fear.

Try to hold the position completely—fingers poised, eyes up—as you say your decoding statements. Don't worry about the wording, and it's okay if you aren't using the statements exactly as you've prepared them. And if you need to rest your eyes, let yourself do so, then gently bring them up again.

Don't overanalyze things. If you get into analysis, it takes you out of the process. If you can't come up with something specific to say, let it be okay to come up with anything that you know you need to let go of. For example:

I decode unrest.
I decode self-doubt.

Step 3: Make a final releasing statement and feel any energetic response.

After your decoding statements, continue to hold your closed eyes upward and keep your fingers in that position for just a moment longer. You have decoded unwanted patterns, so make one last statement, such as *I release it all.*

At this point, take a moment to notice how you feel. You may start to feel a tingling or buzzing on the top of your head, in your forehead, or even in your palms. This is a common reaction, so don't be surprised if it happens. You might also experience some other sensations—perhaps a little light-headedness or feeling like you're floating. Fewer people have felt that way, and some even feel nothing at all. Don't worry about these reactions. They are minor and momentary, leaving as soon as the position is released. And if you don't feel anything, please know that the process is still working anyway.

Step 4: Visualize the release of the old negative patterns moving off to the left.

After you've finished your decoding statements, while still holding the pose with your eyes shut and raised upward, take just a few moments to visualize (or sense) the old negativity that you've decoded drifting out of the left side of your head. You may even see or sense it coming out of your left palm. If you have difficulty visualizing, just *know* it to be moving out to the left, like a cloud drifting farther and farther away. Since the left represents the past, let yourself sense the old, unhealthy stuff floating far, far off to the left, where it disappears and becomes neutral energy. Sometimes people find that as they do this step, their eyes will move off to the left as well. That's fine at this point, because the next step is to let go of the process itself.

Step 5: Drop your hands, release the position, and let all thoughts go.

After you've seen the clouds of negativity completely disappear, let your eyes drop and relax. Take one more deep breath, and on the exhale let your hands drop and let *everything* go. Letting your hands drop disconnects you from this process, and your decoding is finished for this moment in time.

This entire process should take only a few minutes. Take a short break before you go on to the coding process. You can stretch and shake out your hands if you want, but as you get familiar with the process, you will find it easier and easier to move directly to the coding technique. I *highly* recommend that at this point you take a few minutes to write both your impressions and your sensations in your coding journal. You may notice that your emotions are changing already, or it may take the coding process to initiate the emotional change.

Follow-through

Every time you decode, you need to follow it with at least a short session of coding. However, you can also choose to do the coding all by itself. This may sound confusing, but it's kind of like filling a gas tank. Decoding empties the tank, and when your tank is on empty, you have to fill it up. You've emptied your negative thoughts, so coding will fill your mind and your neural pathways with positive new energies. However, you can always add a little more gas (and boost your life energy) by doing the coding as often as you want—even if you haven't done the specific *de*coding. Don't let this mean that you skip the decoding portion completely, though. It's a hugely important part of the overall breakthrough code.

When unhealthy patterns persist, you may need to continue to decode them. So practice this process repeatedly. As long as it takes, it is well worth the effort. When you repeat simple but direct decoding statements and follow them with strong codes, you set a new energetic action in motion in your life.

Having completed the decoding process, you are now ready to code the healthy patterns that replace the false reactions you've let go of. These quantum changes are far-reaching in results, and your action at a distance is beginning to take shape.

CHAPTER 9

THE CODE TO HAPPINESS

"Nothing can bring you peace but yourself."

— Ralph Waldo Emerson

The decoding process described in the previous chapter is the first significant step on the road to profound inner (and outer) happiness. Once you have decoded any reactive pattern, however, it is necessary to code a new, conscious, and healthy one. So always follow the decoding you do with the second component of the breakthrough code—the coding process described in this chapter. It's designed to create and reinforce new patterns of happiness, power, and nurturing responses.

In addition to using this with the decoding, you can also do it on its own or with affirmations and rapid-fire visualization, which are described in Part V. Together the decoding and coding will change your life, but even when used individually, the coding technique can provide amazing emotional shifts that will liberate and empower you.

The Coding Position

Take a moment to look at Figure 2, below. You will no-tice that the person in the drawing is using only her right hand. You can also see that her fingers are placed at the center of her forehead just above the brow line, actually touching her sixth primary energy center.

This is clearly different from what you learned in the last chapter, although it focuses on the same energy cen-ter. The decoding position uses the fingers of each hand and places them on either side of the brow chakra, leaving the space between open. The coding position, however, uses only one hand—the right—and calls for you to place the first two fingertips of that hand *directly* on the energy center itself.

There's an important purpose in this difference. The decoding position runs the energy through the chakra (and the mind) from the right hand to the left, clearing out the old patterns and balancing the hemispheres of the brain. But in the coding position, you are sending the energy directly into the brow chakra—and into the mind, where it is creating new neural pathways and new active, healthy patterns. Energetically, you're igniting the chakra, rewiring the brain, and establishing the positive and powerful responses that you desire to live with.

Here are some tips that will help you engage in a strong and beneficial coding experience:

- Don't worry about the placement of your fingers being exact. Just center the first two fingertips of your right hand above and between your brows, placing them on your forehead there.

- As in the decoding position, you will be raising your closed eyes to "look" upward. If you need to rest them at any point, feel free to do so.

- Don't put too much effort into the process. Just use the position as you say your new emotional intentions. Stressing yourself about doing it the "right way" takes you out of the process itself.

- If you can't remember your exact coding statements, simply say some basic intentions, focusing on power, peace, and positive feelings.

The New Energy Coding Technique

As you can see, this position is relatively easy. Placing the first two fingertips of your right hand directly on your brow chakra is a direct and powerful connection, and over time you will begin to feel a more concentrated energy in this spot. Again, if you find it helpful, you can start by placing your second finger along your brow with your first finger resting against that—as long as the fingertips are directly touching the energy center. Take a few minutes to familiarize yourself with this position before you move on to the steps of the coding process itself.

Step 1: Assume the coding position and close your eyes.

Place your right hand in the position described above, with the tips of your fingers on your brow center. Relax and close your eyes. Take a deep breath and let everything go.

While keeping your eyes closed, raise them slightly, as if you were looking at the very point where your fingertips are touching your sixth energy center. Take just a moment to let yourself feel the energy and power spinning there. You may notice some sensations at the top of your head, in your forehead, or in your palm or fingertips. Many people feel something right from the very beginning, yet for others, it takes several repetitions of the process to experience anything at all.

Step 2: Maintaining this position, say your coding statements.

While holding the position with your eyes closed and raised upward slightly, repeat your coding statements, phrases, and single words. Do some slow, deep breathing as you recite these. The beginning statements reflect the issues you've decoded directly, and they lead on to short, yet more numerous, power statements. For example, if you were responding to the decoding samples from the last chapter, your coding intentions would sound something like this:

I code confidence and peace around other people.
I code peace and trust in the future.

Then you'd go to more specific coding intentions, such as:

I code confidence.
I code strength.
I code peace.

Finally, while still holding the position with eyes closed and looking up, code your strong energy intentions using single words:

Confidence.
Strength.
Power.
Peace.

These single words are an easy, yet important, follow-up to your specific coding statements. The position anchors their energy with strong emotional intention. Such helpful directives can influence any part of your life—so much so, that over time you may even find yourself just using the position and these words to rapidly change your focus and your life in any situation.

Step 3: Upon saying the new codes, notice any physical or emotional sensations and let yourself smile.

As you continue to hold the position with your eyes up and fingers in place, notice any physical sensations that are starting to take place. By this point, you may be feeling stronger buzzing or tingling sensations—or the feeling of floating. These sensations may go from your forehead to the top of your head, or even to the back of your head. You may feel them in the palm of your hand or your fingertips. Although having a physical sensation is not uncommon, the actual feelings are different for everybody. Don't be concerned if you feel a little light-headed; all physical sensations subside soon after the pose is released.

In terms of your emotions, you should be feeling a deeper sense of happiness and a more profound peace within. In fact, this is the one response I hear the most. It brings people peace and even bliss, and makes them feel more powerful and more focused. This will become more natural for you—so automatic, in fact, that it's actually going to cause you to smile. If at first it doesn't, however, let yourself *choose* to smile as you code the powerful intention words. (Even if you don't notice any emotional or physical sensation at all, please know that this step is still working very effectively for you. Over time, you will become more and more familiar with the subtle sensations that accompany this experience.)

Step 4: Affirm the creation of healthy, new neural pathways.

Whatever you may or may not feel, there are important changes taking place. The hemispheres in your brain are balancing, and new pathways of thought and response are being forged. Let yourself acknowledge this valuable shift and affirm the following:

Wonderful new neural pathways are sparking in my mind.

You can phrase the significant changes taking place in any way you want, such as these affirmations:

My brain chemistry is changing for the better.
My subconscious mind is directing healing and creating happiness for me.
My brain is charged with joy.
My mind and life are charged with peaceful and powerful thoughts.

Simply acknowledge that healthy changes are happening in your brain and mind, and know that this experience may go even further. Some people also feel the chemistry in their bodies changing in healthier directions. Let yourself be open to all the levels of healing that can take place. In fact, I often affirm: *My body is producing neurotransmitters of well-being, making me feel joyous and optimistic.*

I have noticed extremely rapid and radical shifts in emotion from doing the coding process even for just a few moments. If I feel too distracted, have too much to do, or have something annoying or frustrating going on in my life, I just stop and do this coding step, stating the specific emotion I want to create at that time. It's amazing how quickly my emotional experience shifts into peace, happiness, focus, or freedom. In fact, I hadn't realized how much I'd been letting little annoyances take me off my happiness track until I started doing this on a regular basis. Now when something agitates me, all it takes is 10 or 20 seconds with my new code, and my happiness returns.

Step 5: Release the coding position. Relax. Embrace and acknowledge your new feelings.

Continue to let the feelings of happiness, peace, and bliss wash over you as you embrace that gentle smile and let go of the coding position. Take a deep breath, relax your eyes into their normal position, and release your fingertips, disconnecting them from your sixth chakra. Let yourself feel the energy, emotion, and positive intention continue to float in your brain, your body, and your personal energy. Relax your shoulders as you drop your hands, shaking them out and stretching your upper body if you feel the need to do so.

Take a few minutes to jot down your impressions in your coding journal. You might want to take note of any physical sensations or shifts in feelings that you have experienced. This is an important part of the process, especially at the beginning. As time goes on, you won't have to do as much record keeping, but for now make sure you write a few words of response to your experience—and perhaps some ideas about what you want to code next.

This coding process should take only a few minutes. Altogether, both the decoding and coding techniques should take no more than three to four minutes when done as the complete Quantum Breakthrough Code. And the time will decrease a bit as you do it more often.

Even though this is a short amount of time, don't be surprised if you feel some pressure in the muscles around your eyes. It's very rare for people to use these muscles on a regular basis. Usually when you have to look up, you do so simply by lifting your entire head rather than keeping your head level and just raising your eyes. For this reason, some people tend to feel a little strain around their eyes or get a bit of a headache when first doing this process. It subsides relatively quickly, but it's still a good idea not to do too many of these sessions all at once, just as you wouldn't spend hours and hours at the gym on your first day back after a long period of inactivity.

I had a friend who was very excited about getting her new codes started, so she spent many hours decoding and coding throughout the night. She ended up with a headache because of the unusual use of the muscles around her eyes. She was fine the next day, but it took her awhile to get back in the swing of things.

So don't overdo it. Take your time and let yourself become accustomed to all the important parts of the process. You will want to repeat these techniques often, just not all at once!

The Coding Continues

I have been using these techniques for a few years now. At the beginning, I had to play with the wording and experiment with different issues. The positions, however, have remained exactly the same since I was given them in that dream. To be honest, there have been times when I didn't notice much of a response. But I kept on with the process, and things really started to click. I'm amazed—even now—by how effective it is.

In fact, something happened tonight as I was writing this chapter. (There are no coincidences.) I received a phone call with some very upsetting information. It was so upsetting that I found myself pacing, with my stomach all tied up in knots. I spent more than an hour like this before I even remembered that I had some options. (We are such creatures of habit!)

The first thing I did was to ask myself if there was anything I could do to change the situation. I knew I could not, but I also knew that I could call someone supportive and vent my feelings. I did that for about ten minutes and then attempted to get back to my writing. I was still too agitated to really focus, and it took me another ten minutes before I realized I could code much healthier responses. I spent about 30 seconds decoding frustration and attachment to the person involved; then I started coding happiness and peace. I had been doing that for only about ten seconds when all of a sudden I started to laugh! I saw so clearly how I let something seem much bigger and much more influential than it had to be. I was happy again. I didn't give a care about that person or situation and knew that it would all unfold exactly as it should—and I would be fine!

Happily, I picked up my writing and finished this chapter, knowing that I was given that wonderfully annoying experience at precisely this time so that I could write about my coding intervention. It's hard to express how liberated and empowered I feel about having this technique at my disposal. I could have gone forward in that annoyed and agitated state for hours—over something I couldn't do anything about! But I am absolutely blissful about being able to feel such significant change and being able to share this with you.

Whatever your initial reaction may be, don't give up and don't dismiss this technique. You deserve to be happy, and you can switch old codes of aggravation into a relaxed and happy consciousness that makes your life a blessing—and puts you in control—no matter what is going on.

As you explore the breakthrough forces in the next section, let yourself identify the changes you want to make. Open yourself to the powerful codes these energies can create. Each force is a very real activator of your personal vibration, able to charge your energy with a radiant resonance that's absolutely irresistible in the energetic realm.

PART IV

THE SEVEN BREAKTHROUGH FORCES

*"Why do you want to open the outside door
when there is an inside door?
Everything is within."*

— **Yogaswami**

CHAPTER 10

THE BREAKTHROUGH FORCE OF SPIRIT

"Our spirit is a being of nature quite indestructible, and its activity continues from eternity to eternity. It is like the sun, which seems to set only to our earthly eyes, but which in reality, never sets, but shines on unceasingly."

— J. W. von Goethe

Your spirit is an intrinsic part of the vast eternal network of Universal energy. Each of us is inextricably connected to all others and to the resonance of the earth through this central identifying energy. And though it is all too easily dismissed, Spirit is at the core of every experience, the source of solution and the epicenter of intention. I believe Spirit is the first, most important force of change.

This dynamic Universal force is a power that moves through space and time and connects us to all others. It's also the force of the seventh energy center, or the crown chakra, which is at the top of the head. As such, it's especially involved in the energetic activity of the coding technique. You may want to dismiss this as being too "mystical," but that's not the case at all. It is energetic in every sense of the word, a constant power that is yours to tap into whenever you so desire.

I have spent most of my psychological and writing career trying to find and understand the energetic reasons behind things, studying everything from consciousness creation to David Bohm's interpretation of quantum mechanics in the theory of interconnectedness, from the functions of neuropeptides and neural transmitters to twin photons and morphogenetic fields. While all these topics are fascinating, and many point to reasons behind the unique experiences of life, there are still unanswered questions. And it seems that some of those questions can only be answered by looking deeper.

Now, there are many scientists who disavow anything existing beyond what we know of the physical world. Yet a seemingly equal number of scientists still firmly believe in the existence of unknown forces—even creative ones. Even Einstein is reported to have said, "Surely something deeply hidden must be behind things."

It's not my intention to try to resolve this debate. I bring it up only to acknowledge that the theories that I talk about in this book, although convincing, are just part of the picture. The other part may be far more compelling. It's a more profound element that exists in the inner knowing that resides within each eternal soul. Some may call it intuition; others may call it faith, or simply a sense of something unknowable. Many feel no need to pursue this line of thinking at all, and if you're one of those people, you may feel free to skip this chapter entirely. After all, the coding technique will still be as powerful and work as well. I have to warn you, though, that you dismiss this information at your own disservice, for this is the one force that is the undercurrent of all experience and has the strength to break through any difficulty at its deepest level.

The Soul as Source

The force of your spirit is integrated throughout your body, your life, your mind, and your very essence as an individual. It's in all the energies and forces that you have at your disposal—and within your deepest nature. So much so that it simply can't be excluded from any part of your life. You may try to deny or dismiss the importance of the eternal spirit within, but it's always present. It's a force to be reckoned with, and it brings important information, power, and direction to your earthly experience.

You are always fully spirit and fully human at the same time. It's easy to feel and understand the human side of your life, but your soul's intentions and hidden directives are a bit more difficult to comprehend. As a result, it's imperative that you create a higher consciousness of your soul and awaken to the code of truth written within. Be aware! This is not just some New Age aphorism. It's the source of your identity and power that transcends the limits that appear to surround you.

Your spirit is one of the grandest forces of all, for it has unlimited creative energy and power in the world. The only constraint comes from refusing to see your soul for the powerhouse it is. Your higher self is the eternal part of you that is, has been, and always will be a destiny co-creator. Combining with the energy and consciousness of your own mind and heart, your soul's intentions help map out your future experiences—as well as bring strength to any present situation.

It may sound strange, but your higher self actually knows more about you than you consciously know about yourself. It's true! Your spirit understands more about what you need and what you're capable of doing than your "personal self" knows. There is a core of information hidden in your soul code that includes the backstory that preceded this life, the deeper meanings of your personal experiences, the real extent of your inestimable value, and the power of all the codes you carry. This is the course of your greatest truth. So if you really want to break through your stuck patterns, awakening to this powerful force is the first place to open up!

The Super Self

The code of your soul comes from your eternal consciousness, originating in Source energy, power, and light. This is the powerhouse of all creation, stemming from the *Oversoul*—the Divine Source—that connects us all in an energetic dance of shared intentions and vibrating consequences. These intentions connect each individual at a higher level and with a greater purpose that goes beyond our personal lives, expanding into global meaning.

In addition, the force of Spirit is charged by the endless helpful and powerful vibrations of the etheric realm, including the loving spirits of family members, friends, angels, guides, and masters. Too many people dismiss this connection in their lives, and they lose infinite power in doing so. I often say that living without the power of Spirit is like never turning on the lights in your home and then cursing the darkness when you bump into the furniture. You go through life without the lights on when you're not connected. Why continue to ignore this dynamic force, cursing your problems, when all along you had the power to tap into the solution?

This Universal force is not just an abstract concept; it's an expansive and powerful vibration. And igniting this energy is more than just turning on the lights. It's opening a vast current of wisdom, guidance, assistance, and love that, like a strong current in a flowing river, can help you move forward and direct you toward the genuine happiness you're longing for.

Spirit on Fire

The force of Spirit is like a rocket engine that, when ignited, sends a missile soaring. And there are many things that you can do to ignite this force and send your own life soaring. In order to do so, however, you need to take this force very seriously. It's the core of your life force, and it can charge all the other breakthrough forces.

Remember, your entire life-force vibration moves out into the Universe, projecting your consciousness into the energetic realm where the seeds of your future reality are sown. The center of that projection—whether you want to believe it or not—is your eternal spirit, the most important and dynamic piece of the puzzle. It's like the core of a nuclear reactor; and if that most important piece were shut down, it certainly wouldn't generate much energy. But you can spark the core of your life force—and project an incredible amount of power and energy that could light up your life like never before.

Igniting Peace

The first ignitor of your spirit is relaxation. In fact, one of the primary ingredients in engaging in this force is the ability (and the willingness) to relax. It may sound weird that you will achieve greater power through peace, but your spirit is charged and offers inspiration through a quiet, open mind and heart. As a result, the regular practice of relaxation is a requirement for igniting this force.

This doesn't mean that the only time you receive inspiration or Spirit-driven power is while you are relaxing. It means that the process of regular relaxation and meditation keeps an open, flowing channel to the energy of Spirit—from the creative and healing energy of the Divine all the way to the Alaya consciousness, the vast field of all the information you will ever need.

The practice of quiet meditation creates a pipeline to your higher self and your intuition, as well as to all the assistance, power, and guidance existing in the energetic realm. So let yourself stop and relax. Take time to meditate. Create quiet and peace in your own heart and mind, and in your environment, too. Start with at least a few minutes of quiet time each day—no distractions, no television or radio, just you, letting go of your thoughts and breathing peacefully into your heart center. Increase your time as you get more comfortable with the process. Let it become a part of your daily life. Make no mistake; meditation is a real tool for both peace and power in your life.

Igniting Your Intuition

Meditating regularly will not only ignite peace but also help you connect with your own intuition. And when it does, you must learn to trust it. Everyone has lots of different voices playing in their heads, including habitual beliefs, fear thoughts, and unending lists of things to do. Some of your more subtle ideas, however, come from your intuitive mind. Although you may have the tendency to give yourself over to the thoughts of your emotional and personal agenda, it's much more important to start listening to your intuition. You may have never realized it, but your intuitive mind has most of the answers you're looking for, and its important guidelines need to be heard and honored.

In order to spark an ongoing practice of intuition, you must first be open to receiving information, and then be willing to trust. Relax, listen to the voice of your own spirit, and let yourself trust and follow the guidance you receive. You can use your coding journal to help you in this process, jotting down any impressions or direction, and noting how each situation turns out.

There are many different types of intuition. *Spontaneous intuition* happens automatically as you're going through your day. It's that fleeting impulse that tells you to take a different way to work, and later you find out that your usual route was closed for repairs. But you can also *direct an intuitive experience* simply by closing your eyes, taking a relaxing breath, and focusing on an issue or question. Ask for the first immediate response, perhaps just a word, an image, or a symbol. Trust what you get, and let yourself be open to the meaning this message brings.

You'll know your intuition by the feel of it. It compels you—but without emotional urgency. If you do feel an emotional urgency, especially something like fear, it's probably your lower feelings directing that thought. Your intuition will never diminish your inner power or your self-love. It will never direct you to do something that doesn't honor you. Your intuitive voice will always ask you to see a higher way and to follow a higher path.

Igniting Spirit Connection and Assistance

In addition to receiving guidance and assistance from your own intuition, you can also get unlimited aid through the spirit helpers around you, through your dreams, and through a deep and open connection with Divine Consciousness. This is such an important and influential force, it's well worth the effort of using the coding technique to create a peaceful mind and receptive and trusting heart. If you feel that your guidance is coming in, but then being blocked by things like your own worry, daily distractions, agitation, or depression, it's important to decode those patterns as well.

So get out of your own way, decode the worry, release the distractions, and always remember to ask. Ask for help or guidance. Ask for healing and strength. Whether you need gentle inspiration or a dramatic solution, ask. I always recommend keeping a notebook by your bed for answers that may come in a dream. In fact, I keep a notebook with me always because I just never know when spontaneous inspiration may come. So ask to receive your answers in a manner that you will understand. Then be open to the messages that come your way.

You *can* build a rapport with Spirit—whether it's the voice of your own higher self, the voice of God, or the loving friends and spirits around you. (Cornelius Vanderbilt sought the advice of a medium before investing in or purchasing companies, and we all know how well he did.) You can achieve these higher levels of consciousness yourself. In time you'll get more and more information from that place of Divine truth and build more trust—not only in your Spirit communication and intuition, but also in the world itself. It's a circle that expands. And your own trust and wisdom will grow exponentially as you continue to ignite this powerful force and make it a part of your everyday routine.

Coding Points

Your ability to relax, your connection with Spirit, and your intuition can all be significant influences in your life. Once they are developed, you can receive information for everything from fleeting, everyday choices to major decisions. To ignite this wonderful force, use the following coding statements when engaging in the techniques you learned in Chapters 8 and 9, and write down any sensations and changes you experience in your coding journal. In fact, remember to call upon your intuition to help you design all your decoding and coding statements!

Decoding:
I decode doubt and disbelief.
I decode stress and agitation.

Coding:
I code a peaceful mind and body.
I code the ability to calm down and relax.
I code comfort with meditation.
I code a peaceful awareness of my own soul.
I code a strong intuition.
I code an open connection to my own spirit and all the loving Spirit energy around me.
I code a clear understanding of the impressions I receive.
I code a willingness to ask and trust.

Are You Blocking Your Energetic Pipeline?

Since relaxation and peace open the door to the many wonderful powers of Spirit, it stands to reason that conflict and disquiet will shut it. In fact, the most common reactive pattern blocking this force is living in agitation. Many people find it difficult to relax because they can't sit still and quiet their mind. This can be a sign of inner conflict, the unending voice of overanalysis, worry, fear, or perfectionism, or just the stress of having too much to do.

The inability to relax and connect could also come from an outer conflict with other people. This can be caused by any level of worrisome unfinished business, unexpressed feelings of hurt or anger, or hostility in the environment—whether at home, at work, or in romance. If this is the case, it will be important to decode and consciously let go of the worry, and calm the inner conflict. Stand up to the hostility and determine what you need to do to resolve things. Make sure that you ventilate your feelings in a journal. Always speak your truth, and know that you deserve to take action on your own behalf.

Difficult times are precisely the times you need to engage the force of spirit most, but your agitated vibration can make it hard for this power to flow. You can decode the agitation and the worry. And when you meditate, ask for Spirit's energy to help you be peaceful and calm—and to give you guidance on resolving any difficulty you may be facing.

Getting Real

Perhaps the biggest block to the force of Spirit is the lack of belief in it. This divisiveness of focus and dismissal of spiritual importance fragments your essential energy, often without your even knowing it. You aren't going to be motivated to meditate or build your intuition if you ignore both the power and the importance of this wonderful force. People live with the physical world, "the real world," in mind. They have the attitude that the energy of Spirit doesn't apply to the real world, and there's no proof of its presence anyway. In addition, those who have been disappointed—perhaps by not having their prayers answered in a specific way—often have lost faith, causing them to break the connection between themselves, the power of Spirit, and their higher self. But it's time to renew your faith in this unseen yet most dynamic power, whatever you define it to be.

In fact, some people's religious experiences or family upbringing actually instilled fear of the spiritual experience. They even have worries about the simple practice of meditation. If this is the case for you, it's important that you decode such apprehension. The anxiety may have come through misinformation in this life or even from persecution in the past. People may say that's crazy, but your eternal code accumulates many specific codes from emotionally charged experiences and reactive patterns you may not understand, nor even know the source of. That's why this process of coding and decoding is so powerful: You don't need to know the source of the problem in order to change it.

Coding Points

Whatever inner or outer conflict may be causing you unrest, don't give up. And try not to be too intellectual for your own good. You can decode your unrest and your resistance. Open up to the power and truth of this amazing force of Spirit within. As you write in your coding journal, let your hand move freely, recording whatever flows onto the page. Use the following statements when doing your coding process to help you get more connected and receive more help from Spirit and your own intuition.

Decoding:

I decode worry and overanalysis.

I decode agitation.

I decode conflict inside and out.

I decode any resistance to opening up to Spirit's love and support.

I decode old patterns of fear.

Coding:

I code comfort and safety in making decisions that honor me.

I code a peaceful heart and a willingness to let go of outer concerns.

I code an easy ability to relax and receive.

I code an open, flowing, receptive connection.

I code a connection to Spirit's love, power, and resolution.

I code the ability to ask for and receive Spirit's assistance in my life.

I code a willingness to connect with my own eternal self.

I code comfort and openness to Divine love and spirit energy.

I code the ability to see all the wonder and power that Spirit has to offer.

Diana's Story

Diana had been raised with lots of misinformation that filled her with fears about many of life's experiences. She used the decoding process to get rid of old traumas and negative feelings and beliefs. She also coded peace, happiness, and self-trust.

The results were subtle at first, but recently became more powerful and more noticeable. Her thoughts are changing in a more positive way, and comforting new ideas just seem to pop into her head—a definite sign of greater intuition and inspiration. And—as often happens when the force of Spirit grows—she has been receiving all sorts of information about everything in her life, including herself, her relationships with others, and her influences from the past. The clarity she's achieved has made her more tolerant of others, more loving toward herself, and much more peaceful in her approach to pretty much everything.

She's much more objective now, seeing a lot of things from her soul's point of view. It's an eternal perspective that brings wisdom and awareness of the deeper meaning of things. Such a viewpoint has a calming effect, reducing striving and perfectionism, and increasing presence, peace, and joy.

Diana acknowledges a much stronger intuitive voice and reports many wonderful experiences of inspiration. That and her calm understanding and clarity are all things that her chronic unrest had made difficult—if not impossible—to achieve before.

Like Diana, you can bring a far greater sense of peace and meaning to your life. Let it be safe and comfortable to connect with Spirit. Open your heart and mind to your own intuition and to the Spirit power all around you. Feel the presence, love, and support that Spirit brings. Relax and affirm: *I am free, open, and aligned to the power and blessings of Divine love and Spirit's abundant gifts. Powerful, vital energy flows through me, bringing me wisdom, healing, and happiness now.* This creates a beautiful life intention!

Quiet your mind and allow yourself to go to that wonderfully peaceful place that starts within and expands to the very ends of the Universe. Once you let yourself receive the love and support of this powerful force, nothing in your life will ever seem the same!

CHAPTER 11

THE BREAKTHROUGH FORCE OF VISION

"Infinite riches are all around you if you will open your mental eyes and behold the treasure house of infinity within you. There is a gold mine within you from which you can extract everything you need to live life gloriously, joyously, and abundantly."

— Joseph Murphy

If you're tired of experiencing the same old feelings and situations, one thing that's guaranteed to help you break through is the powerful force of vision. What exactly is this significant, yet often unconsidered creative element? Well, it starts at the very beginning, with your vision of yourself and of your life. *Everyone* has some sort of view of themselves and their lives, even if they never consciously think about it. *You* are carrying a vision of yourself right now. You might not know it, but you're also carrying a vision of your life and your future.

Take a moment now to ask yourself how you view yourself and your existence. Inwardly, how do you see yourself going through your everyday routine? Do you see yourself as happy-go-lucky, moving through your day with enthusiasm and fun? Consider it carefully, because the vision you carry of yourself and your life is a monumental influence on both your happiness and your destiny creation.

I once posed those questions to a client named Cassie. Of course, her first reaction was to tell me that she'd never thought about it before. But after just a few moments, she said, "I see myself as a pudgy, middle-aged woman who's just going through the motions." Then she added, "But I'm hoping to be happy some day."

We talked about how the force of this previously unspoken vision of herself was laying the groundwork for some continued discouragement and disappointment. She was amazed that although her self-vision was just a quiet undercurrent of her life, it had been a vital part of her chronic assumptions, her inner depressions, and, as a result, her consciousness creation!

In order to change this unspoken yet strong reactive pattern, we went back to her initial core truth—that she had the ability and the power to change things from within. She decoded the negative view of both her life and herself, releasing those images of negativity whenever they came up. She also coded a self-loving vision of herself as an attractive, vital woman who chose to be happy now instead of waiting to be happy "someday."

The results were dramatic. Cassie saw herself—and each day ahead—as joyous, and she started to live in that emotional energy. Slowly she lost the 20 pounds she'd been struggling with for years. She became more active and more social and had more fun, even learning to enjoy a job she had previously found dull.

Mirror, Mirror, on the Wall

The core of a powerful force of vision is a positive view of yourself, and a happy and accepting view of your daily life. This expands to an excited view of your future as well as a positive image of the world you live in. And fortunately, all this can be coded. But if you resist these positive images as being unrealistic, remember the *choice of your vision—* like all the other forces—is ultimately up to you. No matter how negatively you may view yourself, your world, or your future, you do have the option and ability to change that code. You can power up your life with a new code that includes wonderful new images.

Here's an important question: *When you envision your future, whether it's an hour from now, tomorrow, or months or years ahead, how often do you smile?* This may sound silly or irrelevant, but the answer reveals a lot about the force of your vision of your life. Now ask yourself: *What would it take to make me smile at my visions of myself and my future?* Write down your answers in your coding journal.

You can create the image of yourself that you want to be true. See yourself dancing through the activities of your life. Choose a bright, new code and affirm, *I have a wonderful, joyful view of myself, and I choose to have a happy vision of my future.* Use the following ignitors to establish more loving and optimistic views.

Igniting a Wonderful Self-View

Clearly, the first ignitor of this very influential force is a positively charged *view* of yourself. This will seem similar to the positive self-talk or the loving feelings of self, discussed in the next few chapters, but there's an important difference here. This is actually *imaging* yourself with love and joy—and having a tender, accepting reaction when you see yourself in the mirror or in a picture. So be honest, do you have a positive reaction when you see your own image or reflection? If not, it's time to decode that judgment.

This subtle but powerful aspect of thought creates significant shifts, so you must create the conscious intention to have a positive view of yourself—to feel a sense of approval and love at the sight of your own image. This tender visual connection to your identity will lift limitations and create deeper happiness, setting a much higher synchronicity in motion. It's such a genuine and life-affirming energy, it expands your potential in all directions.

So engage in a joyous and much more consciously accepting view of yourself when looking in the mirror. Decode the bits of judgment that may come up about your appearance. Smile, use positive imaging, tell yourself you're beautiful, and blow kisses to yourself. However you want to do it, choose to create a joyful self-regard for your soul's present image. Remember, your spirit is the real source of your beauty, power, value, and worthiness. *Seeing* your soul in the image of yourself aligns you with that truth and with the deepest levels of power that the Universe has to offer.

For this reason, mirror affirmations can be a dynamic part of igniting your vision of self. It may seem simplistic, but this easy practice initiates a life-altering energy! When you look in the mirror and affirm yourself, you create a swirling vortex of energy, projecting your soul truth into the bountiful field of creation. That truth is that you are eternally radiant. As a result, your self-view should never change according to your appearance. In spite of what society would have you believe, your appearance doesn't determine your value or your beauty—your soul does. So no matter what you look like, intend to *see* yourself with love.

To ignite this wonderful force of vision in your life, do the following: First, at every and any image of yourself, let yourself look gently into the eyes and heart of your image and affirm, *I see value there. I see beauty there. I see power there. I see deserving there.* Next, decode critical views of yourself based on your appearance—or on anything else. Code beautiful, light-filled visions of yourself. Code a smiling, happy energy within that shines out to all who view it. Take a few minutes each morning to meditate on this increasingly loving and embracing view—and to code a joyous and accepting vision of yourself. This undercurrent of chosen energy will ignite your vision and trigger a much greater view of your future.

Igniting Images of a Joyful Future

The next ignitor of the powerful breakthrough force of vision is the ability to see fulfillment and happiness in your future. Your life momentum moves in the direction of your inner vision of your future, but like self-view, some people never think about how they *see* their future. Yet if you don't consciously engage in a chosen vision of your future, you could unconsciously engage in a negative view of what lies ahead.

Of course, people visualize their goals all the time, and they visualize themselves being happy upon a goal's completion. However, limiting your future view to just one goal or just one vision could actually sabotage your intentions for success. The subtle message could be that you will only be happy when that goal is completed. This translates into an undercurrent of dissatisfaction about the present that couples with a desperate need to force your goal to happen. Not only is such toxic energy a miserable way to live;

its negative, urgent resonance is also a surefire way to make the future miserable as well.

So what's the solution? Absolutely continue to visualize the successful and happy completion of your goal. Get excited and energized by the prospect, but don't stop there. Your future isn't limited to that one event. Your future is the next moment, the next hour, the next week and month. It's a daily life filled with activity and emotion.

Consciously *choose* a positive view of what your entire future looks like, including joyful daily tasks, relaxing moments, the present steps of getting to your goal, and the happy end results. Don't just envision some unknown moment in time when everything finally works out right. The future is today! Knowing this, you can forge endlessly happy times to come by regularly engaging in a largely optimistic view of the present.

Make it a priority to take a few moments every morning to visualize yourself going through the day ahead. Envision and code happiness. See yourself smiling, making jokes, laughing, singing, dancing, or smelling flowers. Code all these as happy events that help you have a joyful energy and brighten up your life. It is a simple shift that creates an irresistible resonance.

Whatever you have to do today, see yourself taking every opportunity to do it with joy. If this vision seems foreign to you, decode the dread and negativity with which you have come to view your daily life. Code bliss and appreciation instead. When you continue to code a new sense of freedom and joy, you will see those energies become stronger forces in your life!

Ask yourself what you can do right now to make your joyous visions a reality. You may have been filled with negative views of yourself and of your future, but remember that these don't have to be true for you anymore. In fact, they're really just false, yet deeply indoctrinated, assumptions. Only you can determine how you view yourself and your life. No matter how you came up with your perception, you have the option to change it now. The reactive patterns that are blocking your clear and truthful view can be decoded, and your new code can unlock the powerfully creative force of vision that turns wonderful potential into reality!

Coding Points

In order to activate these beneficial practices and ignite the force of vision in your life, use the following statements in your process. Remember to support your Quantum Breakthrough Code with all the lifestyle changes suggested, and use your coding journal to help yourself stay on track. If the positive visions are difficult for you, you can code the ability and the desire to do them every day.

Coding:
I code the power to choose my own view.
I code joy and happiness in my own self-vision.
I code the ability to visualize each day with joy and beauty.
I code the ability to live with joy each day.
I code a light-filled view of my future and the world.
I code total self-love whenever I see an image of myself.
I code joyous images of myself and each day ahead.

Dark Visions

Let's examine the common reactive patterns that block this generating force of vision. It's clear that the first block is a negative self-view. You may have a sad and ugly image of yourself that derails the strength of *all* your visualizations. You may see yourself as not good enough, not attractive enough, or perhaps not young enough, but these are not your truths—no matter how convinced you are of them. You must decode these negative views and see yourself in an entirely different light—the light and vision of your eternal self.

A powerful meditation is to see yourself bathed in glowing energy, sending out a brilliant and beautiful light to the Universe for all to see. And whenever you see your reflection in a mirror, visualize radiance in your heart and all around you. Smile (yes, do it) at your own powerful and eternal light.

To spark up your view of yourself, affirm: *I view myself with love and appreciation. Every time I pass a mirror, I smile and see the light and beauty of my soul.* Make sure you code this new pattern as a natural reaction to your vision of yourself, and know that you deserve to embrace this truth.

Decoding Her Own Dark View

You may recall my client Peggy, who had several issues to deal with. A significant one was her negative view of herself. She had labeled herself as unattractive long ago. Her parents had compared her to her sisters and had always found her lacking. So now she constantly compared her looks to others, seeing them as prettier, younger, more stylish, and so on. This was a totally self-destructive code that needed to be eradicated. So we worked on decoding that view, along with some other patterned assumptions of self-judgment, an important reactive pattern that will be explored more deeply later in the book.

Peggy coded loving self-acceptance along with the ability to see herself as attractive no matter what her inner voice might say. She also intervened on all the thoughts that had plagued her about her appearance. I spoke to her recently, and she told me, "For the first time in my life, I looked in the mirror and I actually thought I was beautiful! I really felt it, and I could *see* it, too!"

Her vision was genuine and heartfelt—and a complete 180-degree shift. It brought tears to my eyes. She coded a new vision, and it became the way she actually viewed herself. Her external life was changing, too. She was forging more friendships, and people were responding to her differently. She learned that the world sees you as you see yourself.

Future Falling Short?

When you get your self-view in shape, it's time to look at how you see your future. A bleak but common block to the force of vision is a pervasively negative view of the world and of the days to come. Some people actually see and sense the planet as a dark place, and if you're one of them, you need to decode that habit and lighten up the picture. When you go out, see the beauty surrounding you. Visualize light around the people you meet—as well as around yourself. Bring color and joy to your images of the world and code more joy in your vision of the time to come.

When it comes to your future, start with today. Decode any negative view of the activities ahead, and code a new habit of seeing the potential fun and joy in everything you have to do. Also decode any fear of the future, and code happy and optimistic images of the time to come.

Visualize your goals front and center. This placement is important because whether your desire is left, right, or in the distance, it indicates to your subconscious mind how far you have to go in order to get to that goal. See the day ahead—and all the time in front of you—filled with light, happy events, and images of enjoyable experiences.

Coding Points

In order to activate the powerful force of vision, use the following statements to decode your blocking reactive patterns and to code a bright, new view. Note your progress in your coding journal.

Decoding:

I decode negative views of myself.
I decode any dark views of my future or the world.
I decode old patterns of worrying about how people see me.

Coding:

I code happy, smiling energy.
I code loving and attractive views of myself.
I code acceptance of my appearance.
I code the ability to see happiness everywhere I go.
I code value in my vision.
I code the ability to see my life and my goals with joy.
I code the freedom to choose a lovely vision of myself and my future.
I code powerful, happy views.

Tanya's Travels

I recently received a wonderful e-mail from a woman who lives in England. Tanya has suffered from a driving phobia for many years. She found it difficult to drive outside her comfort zone, having a lot of fear whenever she had to drive to unfamiliar surroundings or far-off places.

This, like most phobias, comes from a catastrophic view of the future. In fact, most people with phobias automatically go to the worst-case scenario regarding their particular fear and picture it in terrible detail. It's a gripping and uncomfortable reactive pattern, and Tanya was ready to let it go.

After taking the online seminar where I taught the Quantum Breakthrough Code, she used it to address what had been limiting her for so long. After a few weeks of doing the decoding and the coding, she felt ready and confident to challenge her fear. She invited a couple of her friends to drive with her to Oxford, which is an hour's journey from her home. In the past she would have never done that. Or if she forced herself to, she would have been anxious, thinking that something horrible might happen on the journey or that she might get lost or make a mess of things. This time she felt very comfortable driving—with no worries or fearful thoughts—and everything seemed to go just right for her.

In fact, one of her friends suggested that they drive even farther to tour a church that was another 15 minutes away. If this had happened just a few weeks before, Tanya would have fallen into a panic, frantic about not being able to find the place and getting lost. But this time she thought that the Universe was giving her another opportunity, and she suddenly felt very comfortable and excited about going somewhere entirely different. She was thrilled not only about the new discovery, but also about her new calm feelings.

And when she and her friends arrived, they found a wonderful old church with a stunning view and a beautiful, massive old tree in its yard. Later, she found herself driving easily and effortlessly back to Oxford and then back home. It was a long but exciting day, and it was such a total reversal of her previous experiences that Tanya said the result was a miracle to her.

I was so happy to receive Tanya's e-mail. It's always such a wonderful feeling to be liberated from old fears and limitations. It seems that anxieties and phobias—like so many other issues—are especially treatable with the decoding and coding technique. If these are present for you, here are some sample statements that Tanya used for her particular case. You can do something similar, addressing your own specific fears—or you can use your intuition to create the statements that are best for you.

Decoding:

I decode fear and insecurity while driving my car to unfamiliar places—especially in the dark.

I decode fear of getting lost when I'm driving my car to unfamiliar places.

I decode fear when I'm driving.

I release it all.

Coding:

I code safety and confidence when I drive my car to places I'm not familiar with.

I code a strong sense of safety and security when driving my car any time of the day.

I code confidence and safety when I'm driving my car.
I code safety. I am safe.
I code confidence. I am confident.
Confidence.
Security.
Safety.

If you're living with fear or any sad view of the future, you can create a new code. You are the one who paints the pictures in your mind, and the process is going on right now. You have the power to make your images beautiful, so do it. It totally shifts your life force—and your results—when you fill the world and the future with the beautiful pictures in your head. Affirm: *I see my life as a happy adventure. My days and my future are filled with the light of love and joyous activity, and my world is filled with beauty.*

When you choose to see the value and beauty of both your inner light and your outer reflection, your life force resonates with your soul's truth. Decode any resistance to this truth, and code the choice to see yourself in the light and love and joy that you deserve. Do this often, and before too long, you'll also *see* some wonderful new experiences coming your way.

CHAPTER 12

THE BREAKTHROUGH FORCE OF EXPRESSION

*"How can a bird that is born for joy
sit in a cage and sing?"*

— **William Blake**

The third force that is supremely capable of breaking through stuck patterns is *expression,* the ongoing energy that resonates with the highly influential vibration of how you communicate to yourself and others. The flow of healthy communication can clearly impact your personal, professional, romantic, and even physical experiences. And this isn't limited to the spoken word, but includes your thoughts, writings, body language, and all other ways that you express yourself, your ideas, and your emotions.

Most people aren't aware of the momentum that their expression generates. The thoughts you say to yourself are electromagnetic in nature, and what you say out loud amplifies that with an acoustic resonance. This creates a quantum vibration that never stops broadcasting your self-dialogue outward to the Universe. But if you never stop to consider how and what you're expressing—on a day-by-day basis—it will be really hard to control your emotional and personal destiny. And if you're not communicating at all, you may unknowingly be locking yourself in the cage of a joyless life.

It's a fundamental truth that how and what you express becomes a significant part of your personal code. After all, expression, like vision, is a constant—and usually unconscious—activity in your daily life. Therefore, it's time to become more aware of these habits. When you read through the blocking reactive patterns, make it a priority to decode the ones you most frequently engage in. Also remember to code the following ignitors of dynamic expression. Building a clear, healthy way of expressing yourself will establish powerful codes of communication that will expand your intentions immeasurably.

Igniting Powerful Self-Talk

The first ignitor of this vibrant breakthrough force is honoring and optimistic self-talk. What you say to yourself and how you do it is, in my opinion, the biggest influence on your ability to be happy. As such, it's also an intrinsic part of your life-force energy, weaving your words into the very vibration of your self-esteem and your potential peace of mind. Both of these influence the emotion of self-love, which is at the core of your eternal code. Like a beautiful self-vision, when your self-treatment and self-expression are filled with love, compassion, and a high self-regard, they create a powerful vortex that resonates with your eternal truth and rings out to the world with radiant joy and vitality. These genuinely happy vibrations are irresistible to the Universe by virtue of your sacred alignment with your own eternal truth.

For this reason, loving self-expression has to be an ongoing priority that you approach in two significant ways:

1. Intervene on and decode your negative self-talk. When you catch yourself speaking negatively to yourself—whether it's about you or virtually anything else—make a conscious choice to release that negative self-talk. Decode the habit of negativity. Then gently code optimistic and honoring options.

Throughout this book you have been encouraged to decode patterns of negativity, and self-expression is no exception. Fearful or critical self-talk generates such pervasive unhappiness, it needs to be decoded as often as possible. But do this lovingly, without faulting yourself or worrying about what it all means. Just let it go and choose the positive code of peace, trust, and self-encouragement instead.

2. Make a habit of coding loving, optimistic self-expression. Code your intention to be more affirmative more of the time. This isn't just lip service; it's embracing the truth of your power and value in the words of your own mind and heart. And the act of coding will take your affirmations deep into the cellular level. It activates a new pattern of responses, thereby rewiring neurons in a positive way. This energetic approach establishes truthful and empowering expression in the depths of your being.

As you'll see in the next chapter, the force of love is within your core eternal code, but it may take some time and determination to indoctrinate the wonderful *expression* of it into your personal life. Code a greater love for yourself—and in the way you express that love to the world.

In doing so, you will be breaking through blocks that may have been lodged in the energy centers of your mind and your throat, which is the fifth chakra, the center of expression. Clearing this energy center opens the way for greater things to be thought and said about you by others as well.

Igniting Healthy Expression to Others

Our expression reaches out from us and connects with people and the world in truly dynamic ways. This is such an influential piece of the puzzle, it should come as no surprise that the next ignitor of this powerful force is a clear and peaceful expression to others. Each of us lives with a layered and complex belief system about ourselves, other people, the world, the economy, and all manner of things. The intricacy of this belief system—and our view of our connection with others—will have a strong influence on our approach to them.

Some people tend to approach others with arrogance or anger. Many perceive others with fear. And there are lots of folks who just shut down and tend not to communicate at all. None of these approaches are healthy forms of expression.

Of course, you still need to vent your difficult emotions in appropriate and healthy ways. But just as it's dishonoring to stuff down your feelings, it's equally unhealthy to live in a constant state of raging and blaming. If it seems that this is one of your patterns, you need to know that it does *not* give you power; it only takes power away. So let yourself decode any chronic complaining and abrasive expression, and code greater comfort and clarity in your communication to others.

Whatever the situation, healthy expression is civil, clear, and self-honoring. It releases judgment and the need to manipulate. And loving expression is filled with compassion and appreciation. When we realize that statements of hope, optimism, and peace expand those energies in our lives, we will choose to engage in them more and more.

This doesn't mean you have to be passive. For you to really ignite the force of expression, it will be important to break through your passive patterns. Real happiness doesn't come from avoiding conflict; it comes from speaking your truth and knowing you have the right to do so. So the act of peaceful expression doesn't mean maintaining the peace at all cost; it means establishing the pervasive sense of calm that comes from knowing who you truly are and being willing to express that to anyone and everyone.

Igniting Truthful Talk

This brings us to the next ignitor, which is the act of speaking your truth—both to yourself and to others. This may be difficult for those who have no idea of their true power or valuable identity. If you feel lost in this area—or just confused—it's time to call upon the deeper code of your soul self. Speaking your truth comes from opening to that eternal identity and being willing to acknowledge your worthiness from that place. This takes courage because it requires a willingness to ask for what you want and know that you deserve it.

If you refuse to speak your truth, you're dismissing your own power, always holding yourself back, biding your time, longing for recognition, and waiting to be fulfilled. Your life becomes coded with deep feelings of unfulfillment and lack of joy. Frustration abounds because you're unable to ask for or even express what you need. Eventually, these emotions build to the point of boiling over, creating codes of agitation or depression that reign supreme.

When this happens, the magical flow of the current of truth and expression simply moves around you, leaving you behind. This is so important that it often becomes a life lesson in learning how to speak your truth. So if you have difficulty standing up for yourself, expressing your emotions or opinions, or making reasonable requests on your own behalf, you need to decode those old, stuck patterns. Decode the habit of shutting down, and code the comfort and courage to open up.

Say It Loud, Say It Strong!

The coding technique is a process of expression, and using powerful words is one of the most dynamic ways to energize and accelerate this force. As discussed earlier in the book, you'll find that the best coding statements evolve in form from simple but dramatic statements to phrases and single words. Code with words of power and unlimited truth, and when you do, recognize their innate vibration in your life-force energy.

This approach shifts your focus from the details of whatever issue you may be working on to something more direct and more emotional in intention. And you can actually code this new practice throughout your day by using the steps from Chapter 9 and saying: *I code the ability to choose words of power and grace.* Then simply say: *I code power. I code grace.*

You can also design your coding expressions to fit the situations you're in. For example, if you're feeling anxious or afraid, you can decode those emotions and next code comfort and present peace. Then put these words into your daily lexicon. Coding power states such as joy, strength, and freedom in your daily way of speaking to yourself will create an entirely new experience of life.

All these energies are already vibrating in your eternal code, and in truth you *are* unlimited in your value and your power. It's your choice now to become unlimited in your comfort, joy, and freedom, too. It is *all* within you. All you have to do is decode the old expressions of limitation and reawaken to the wonderful unlimited code of truth within.

Coding Points

If you want to charge your life with the powerful force of healthy and focused expression, use the following statements in your coding process. Affirmations are also wonderful ignitors of this force. Use your intuition and make wonderful expression a priority. Sing out your truth!

Decoding:

I decode habits of negative self-talk.
I decode self-criticism.
I decode fear and self-loathing.

Coding:

I code positive and accepting self-talk.
I code clear and comfortable expression.
I code loving words that support me.
I code comfort in talking to others.
I code the ability to speak my truth.
I code power.
I code peace.

Say What?

It's clear how the reactive pattern of self-negation can be a monumental block to truthful expression (and to many of the other breakthrough forces). This is so important that it must not be dismissed! No matter how firmly convinced you are that your negative self-talk is true, you have to remember: It does *not* make you happy; it does *not* project a magnetic energy; and it does *not* represent the inherent truth of the eternal, worthy, valuable, and powerful spirit that you are.

You simply cannot fudge on this. Your inherent definition of yourself is one of your most deeply indoctrinated codes and one of the biggest sources of both the degree of happiness and the quality of the resonance in your life. So whenever you realize that you're devaluing yourself or your life in any way, jot it down and put it in your coding journal on the list of items you want to decode.

If you intend to achieve, you need to talk to yourself with encouragement. If you intend to be respected, you must code respectful self-talk. And if you intend to feel attractive, you have to acknowledge how wonderful and attractive you are. So investigate your self-talk through this question: *Does the code of my self-talk match the positive vibration of my personal intentions?* If not, you must change it. The coding technique can transform your inner dialogue, bringing real happiness and real results.

Lovingly forgive yourself for any self-criticism, and decode it. And please don't criticize yourself for criticizing yourself—that just deepens the negative code! Instead, gently choose a different path. Code the ability to choose healthier and more honoring statements. Intervene on self-doubt as often as possible, and then code the choice to express and embrace your wonderful truth. Open your heart and mind to that new code of loving self-definition, one in which you accept yourself just as you are and speak to (and about) yourself and your life with deep appreciation.

Afraid to Say . . .

The next reactive pattern blocking the powerful force of expression is fear—both of confrontation and of standing up for yourself. Fear of conflict often grows out of a history of hostility from others—especially when you've tried to express yourself but been met with anger. Receiving such aggression only causes you to be more nervous and more afraid of speaking up for yourself. Rejection, or even just upsetting someone, feels very risky—so much that you may prefer to sacrifice your own power and happiness just to avoid having a confrontation.

If this is something you experience, you need to begin by taking little risks in expressing yourself. Decode your fear and your old willingness to dismiss your own needs. Then act with—and code—more and more courage and comfort in speaking up. Know that you have the right and the power to stand up for yourself. And in fact, if you don't prioritize yourself in this way, you're not going to attract the kind of relationships or situations where you're a priority for others.

This is an entrenched reactive code for many people, so it's important to let yourself move through this at your own pace. Allow yourself to observe the pattern, making little changes and building on them. Code the desire and the ability to express yourself—no matter how others may react. *What others think or do can no longer be a guiding factor in your expression.* So decode any fear of their responses and make it a priority to code a new sense of courage, safety, and the freedom to speak. If you don't take action here, the results can often lead to the next difficult reactive pattern, totally *shutting down,* a deep and consuming energy block.

Lights Out!

Shutting down is quite a common reaction when emotions run high and people fear potential confrontation. The presence of strong negative energy compels many to deny, ignore, dismiss, or simply pretend that something uncomfortable is *not* happening. The need to "keep the peace" builds a habitual code of shutting up in the hope that things will settle down and be manageable again. But without expression, this is a false sense of peace. Shutting down actually results in shutting *out* life!

You may be adept at burying unexpressed emotions deep within, but the vibrations of those experiences linger. It's a code of apprehension that makes you feel unsure and unsafe, affecting your comfort and your life force significantly. Remember, such debilitating codes dominate your emotional life as well as the consciousness you project to the world. So keep this in mind: If you're shutting down your own expression, you're also shutting yourself down to the grateful expression from the Universe!

It may feel risky at first, but as you decode the fear of confrontation, it will become easier to face your feelings— even if they are difficult. Venting old feelings of pain and anger, along with releasing present hurts, will help you express yourself in healthy ways. Using a journal, whether your coding journal or another notebook, to get things out will bring clarity to your energy and power to your personal process. All of this is a part of creating a new code of expression, and it's certainly better than holding it all in.

People shut down in a lot of different ways. Some can't ever talk about their feelings. Others shut down only when around certain individuals, perhaps their parents or other authority figures. Some people are fine with their friends but can have a difficult time at work. It varies depending on your comfort level and your history.

So investigate any patterns you may have of shutting down. Whatever form the reaction may take, let yourself identify and decode the patterns and feelings that cause you to do so. You may have to work on this consistently if it is a deep indoctrination for you. However, you can code comfort in practicing speaking up. Code a willingness to take the risk of being open and expressive. Code peace and freedom in telling your truth.

Angry Words

The last reactive pattern is the opposite of shutting down (but often has that effect on others). Although hostile expression, which includes rage and anger, seems less common, there are still many people who live in this agitated energy. They're often loud, abrasive, agitating, power mongering, arrogant, or continually angry.

Although anger expressed appropriately is healthy, this kind of ongoing, agitating energy can actually block your authentic expression. Chronic anger reveals a deep code of dissatisfaction, which is a strong negative filter in your life. This creates a ragged energy that agitates your vibrational projection to the world. And be aware: Some people think anger brings power, but it actually reduces your power—coding difficulty for you personally, and drawing it back to you from the Universe.

Although it's difficult to admit to this habit, it's an important part of your process. Genuinely happy and confident people never need to be hurtful or demeaning power mongers. In fact, both the energies of hostile expression and no expression at all (shutting down) are based in fear, and this lack of authentic happiness makes it next to impossible to break through any persistent present problems.

So be honest about your agitation levels. Where does your anger really come from, and what do you want to do with it? Do you want to live in this abrasive code or let it go? Use your coding journal to explore these questions, and note the emotions and energy you notice. You can decode and release patterns of excessive anger or mean-spiritedness. Code the ability to stay calm and express yourself with peace. Let go of the bravado, and see the world as safe, comfortable, and even fun. In fact, *whatever* difficulties you may have with communication, make sure you always code fun. The attitude and energy of playfulness is a simple but powerful *expression* of your joy.

Coding Points

If you find yourself withholding your honest and honoring expression, you may be finding a lot of stuck patterns in your life. This force—when blocked—can affect every arena, from career and success to love and romance. Use the following statements to decode any negative patterns, and let your life force harmonize with the world around you.

Decoding:

I decode worry about what people think.
I decode any fear of confrontation.
I decode responsibility for others' feelings.
I decode irritability and angry responses.
I decode the habit of shutting down (at work, around my parents, and so on).
I decode fear and hesitation.

Coding:

I code comfort and peace in speaking up (to Mom, Dad, my boss, and so on).
I code the courage to speak up in any situation. It is my right.
I code the ability to express my sense of my own value.
I code the ability to be peaceful and loving in my self-talk.
I code comfort in expressing myself.

Kelly's Expressive Career

The fear of public speaking is one of the most common phobias in America today. Yet it's also one of the most easily transformed reactive patterns when using the Quantum Breakthrough Code. I've heard from so many people who had been filled with fear, yet found more comfort and calm after engaging in this process. Kelly was one of those people, and her story is inspiring in many ways.

Kelly was embarking on a new career that was both challenging and very exciting for her. She was taking a class to learn how to become a medium, someone who receives messages from Spirit and then relays those messages to individual clients or people in an audience. This required peace and trust in both herself and in her process, and she was happy when she received the messages successfully. There was one significant obstacle, however. She knew that, in time, she would have to take her career to the next level, doing public demonstrations.

Just the thought of it made Kelly sick. When she tried working in public in the past, she had all sorts of symptoms, including wanting to run out of the room. So she decided to get rid of this old code once and for all. She decoded fear of public speaking and fear of what others thought. She then coded confidence when speaking in public. She also coded trust in herself, love, and self-acceptance. And she coded peace in any situation.

When the evening of her demonstration for class grew near, Kelly felt more comfortable than ever before. She was a little nervous, but the sick feelings were gone. She kept wondering why she didn't feel like running out of the room. When her turn came, she stood up with complete confidence in front of a room full of people. She gave her messages, and her instructor told her that she had done great and didn't need to change a thing.

Kelly was happy and excited. A classmate even told her that she looked as though she'd enjoyed it. She knew that she had beat the old uncomfortable pattern, but the real proof came two weeks later when she got an e-mail from her teacher, asking her to do her public message work again, which she did.

Kelly now has the knowledge that she can take on this task any time she wants. She is free from the old code of fear that was so strong, it was blocking her greatest desire. Now she can express herself fully and freely, and her new code of peace and self-trust is bringing her fulfillment and deep feelings of success.

You, too, can decode your blocks to expression. They may not be public, but they are worth your attention. Release the old patterns that are stopping you from speaking your truth and expressing your needs, and code comfort and confidence in all that you say.

Your words move out from you in clear directives to the Universe. When you hold them in or change them to fit someone else's needs, you sabotage your own intentions for real happiness and success. It's time to be your authentic self in all you say and do. Know that you are free to say something new to yourself, to express the love and joy that are waiting to be spoken. Live in the undeniable truth that you deserve to express your value to the world. You are a part of the symphony of life; let the music of your soul join in!

CHAPTER 13

THE BREAKTHROUGH FORCE OF LOVE

"What is life without the radiance of love?"

— J. C. Friedrich von Schiller

It's the subject of countless songs and poems. It's the theme of novels and movies, the source of great joy and equally consuming angst. Yet beyond all this, the *force* of *love* is one of the most influential energies in the world.

Many people consider this a cliché. They talk about the emotion of love and about the consciousness field of love. There's so much talk about loving energy, it actually diminishes its credibility and power in the minds of many. But it's important to realize that love is a moving, fluid, viable force in the Universe. It's one of the strongest and most productive, aligning both the creative force of Universal intention with the power of your own personal emotion of love.

Pure love, when measured with muscle testing, also known as kinesiology, registers at one of the highest vibrational rates. As a result, it magnetizes the best things to you. And when love is purely projected, it resonates with the strength of your own Divine consciousness—not just the God consciousness outside of you, but your *own* Divine consciousness as well. All the breakthrough forces and positive energies you can engage are accelerated by the power of love. Starting with Spirit all the way through the forces of vision, action, and responsibility, the presence (or lack) of love colors every experience you have.

Burnin' Love

There are many ways to ignite the force of love. Use affirmations on a regular basis to bring greater love to yourself. Treat yourself kindly and engage in happy pursuits. Surround yourself with things and people you care about. These are all good ways to start. But as with the last two breakthrough forces, the source of real power starts within. Like expression and vision, the vortex of this force ignites when you *choose* to give love to yourself.

Igniting Self-Love

The first ignitor of love is *self*-love, which is necessarily at the core of all types of love. This Universal force is awakened and energized when you embrace your eternal identity and view your worthiness through your sacred Source. You become so empowered when you live in this vibration; and conversely, it's impossible to be truly happy when you live in the energy of self-doubt or self-hate.

It's important to start with the knowledge that you *deserve* to love yourself and treat yourself lovingly. Many people can agree with this intellectually but have difficulty feeling it in their heart of hearts. But the fact is, you deserve *all* love—your own, that of others, and Divine love, too.

Unfortunately, most people aren't taught how to do this, so they must *learn* how to bring this energy to themselves. And if you're one of these individuals, you need to make this a high priority. Loving yourself is neither selfish nor arrogant. It is, instead, a clear choice to see and acknowledge the beautiful soul within—and to cherish that part of you that transcends time and mundane experiences.

If loving yourself seems to be an issue for you, it will be necessary to code a self-accepting and self-forgiving attitude. This calls for you to accept and approve of yourself without limitation or condition. And if you feel you've done something that you're not quite proud of, it's important to let go and code forgiveness. No matter what you may feel guilty or ashamed about, you deserve your own forgiveness and unconditional acceptance. Until you give this to yourself, it's unlikely that the force of love will flow freely in your life—and equally unlikely that you will receive what you long for from others.

In fact, without self-love and self-acceptance, you're always going to see yourself as faulty in some way. This makes the world a hostile and unwelcoming place. Fearing that you're being judged, you'll always strive for others' approval simply because you refuse to give it to yourself. So to ignite love's power, it will be very important to decode all old patterns of self-criticism and self-judgment and to code the belief that you are worthy, equal, valuable, and deserving.

This core of self-acceptance is what makes you truly relaxed, happy, and magnetic. It's a life-force vibration that unleashes Universal love in such a significant way that it shifts the way you experience everything. Whatever else you may be using this technique for, also code genuine feelings of self-love and compassion for who you are inside.

This will accelerate change on all levels and help activate the next ignitor of love as well.

Igniting Love for Others

An extension of your own harmonious energy can be seen in the next igniting force: love and compassion for others. Forging more peaceful connections brings greater synchronicity into your life, one that will spark a network of magical events! Combining love of self with love for others projects a profound energy of trust and happy expectations. There's an accelerated shared intention when people release judgment and engage in mutual acceptance, patience, and understanding. Treatment of self is inextricably linked to the treatment of others, and when you cultivate kindness for others *along with* compassion for yourself, it weaves a tapestry of harmonic resonance for all.

Of course, you still need to be discerning about whom you spend your time with and how you interact with them. Self-honoring is always the highest choice and should be your primary approach, but you can still bring a greater reverence to everything and everyone around you. And this kind of respectful love has the power to break through any block!

Coding Points

No matter how you feel now, you can code a deep and abiding love for yourself. Coding more tolerance and acceptance of others will help you tap this energy as well. Use these statements as you do your coding process. Notice any other loving patterns you want to add to your life, and write them down in your coding journal.

Decoding:

I decode self-negation.
I decode feelings of unworthiness.
I decode impatience with myself or others.

Coding:

I code an accepting and loving attitude toward myself.
I code a tender feeling for myself.
I code a high regard for myself and my worth.
I code a clear sense of my true eternal value.
I code loving self-forgiveness.
I code a deep sense of deserving.
I code unconditional self-love and self-acceptance.
I code tolerance and patience with others.
I code love for myself and others.
I code love for my life and for the world.

Stop, in the Name of Love!

If the first ignitor of this powerful force is self-love, then the first blocking reactive pattern is self-loathing or self-dismissal. Such feelings of inadequacy are enormous blocks that stop you cold, not only because they're negative, but also because they simply are *not* your truth. I've seen this mistake over and over again throughout my psychological practice. People willingly embrace the negativity of their parents as being unquestionable, bringing them misery and frustration that can run throughout their lives.

These programmed feelings are based on false beliefs, and they must be decoded! Just because you *feel* inadequate doesn't mean that you *are* inadequate. You may have been living according to the lies that someone else has present-ed to you, but now it's time to decode those assumptions of inadequacy, self-judgment, and self-hatred. It's time to open yourself to your soul's unassailable truth that you are eternal, strong, valuable, and deserving of your own acceptance and love.

Feelings of unworthiness or undeserving create a very low, dense current that not only makes you miserable, but also severely darkens your energy. But even self-loathing codes can be changed, and you have the power to code the certain knowledge that you are valuable and deserving of love and of all the great and wonderful things the world has to offer!

You can choose to become your own loving parent, your own loving friend. Stop many times throughout your day to take a few moments to code self-encouragement and feelings of self-love. If you want those things from others, you must give them to yourself.

One Is the Loneliest Number

The magnificent force of love is often blocked by isolation and separation. Our disconnect from others is many times based in fear or envy, and it can make a person miserable. Fear of others can come in the form of being hurt or worrying about what they think. Or you may judge yourself as you assume they would judge you. You might even need to impress them or make them feel inferior in order to feel good about yourself.

All this comes from a pervasive win-lose mentality that can take you out of your peace and harmony by creating never-ending striving. This toxic and self-sabotaging code is all too prevalent. For real peace, decode the toxic patterns of envy, fear, and competition. Choose to connect with others on a heart-to-heart basis instead. Know that the abundant Universe can provide for all, and all are deserving—including you. Your old codes of competition only divide you from others and block up your force of love. This takes you out of the flow of Universal synchronicity, filling you with envy and making others' blessings and acceptance seem distant and unattainable.

Coding Points

The patterns of our lives build a momentum all their own, and the habit of self-negation is one of the strongest and most impeding blocks to happiness. Use the following coding statements to break through. Also decode feelings that the world is a threatening place where your value is held in comparison to others. Code equality and peaceful feelings instead.

Decoding:

I decode self-dismissal.
I decode limitation and judgment.
I decode fear of others.
I decode any sense of inequality.
I decode envy.
I decode comparison and competition.
I decode inadequacy.
I decode striving.

Coding:

I code freedom and self-respect.
I code a deep sense of my own value.
I code a deep love for myself—now and always.

I code a willingness to feel the unlimited wonder, power,
  and value within.
I code the power to believe in myself.
I code the knowledge that I am worthy.
I code a deep sense of equality to all others.
I code tolerance and patience with myself and others.
I code loving connections.
I code grace and peace.
I code love.

Decoding Attachment: Melany's Forgiveness

There are many types of relationships, and we can forge unending codes around all our connections to others. One of the most impeding of these codes is attachment, and it can hold on for years. Attachment to another doesn't only come in the form of longing. It can also come in the form of hurt, anger, and rejection.

This is what happened to a client named Melany, who had suffered terrible abuse in her childhood and teen years from members of her extended family who had been hurtful, cold, and intimidating to her. Over and over again, they had made it clear that she was unworthy and brutally rejected her. For decades, Melany carried pain, anger, and even fear of them. She had extreme anxiety whenever she was around them, so she eventually stopped seeing them altogether.

When Melany learned the decoding and coding techniques, she decided to address this issue. She kept her statements simple and brief, coding things like self-love, but focusing on forgiveness—forgiveness for those who hurt her, but also for herself. As soon as she started the process, she felt lighter and pleasantly optimistic.

She did this coding on a regular basis but not every day. After a while, she found herself meeting up with these people whom she hadn't seen in years. They were visiting a sick relative, and it was totally unexpected.

This time when she walked into the room, the energy was completely different. She felt far less intimidated than she ever had before. She even felt confident and free, totally opposite emotions to the ones she had when she'd been negatively attached. In fact, she also felt compassion for the elderly people who had been so hurtful to her for so long.

And not only did *she* respond differently, but so did they. For the very first time, they were actually happy to see her. One asked for a hug, and another told Melany that she loved her. She had gotten more kindness and affection from them in those few minutes than she had received in her entire childhood and adolescence.

She recently saw them again, and the one relative who had been particularly haughty and mean looked right at her and expressed how much she loved her. Melany sees this reversal—both in her comfort and freedom and in their treatment of her—as miraculous. But just as crucial is the fact that her belief in what forgiveness is has radically changed. She used to think it meant condoning mistreatment. Now she knows that it's releasing yourself and your transgressor from that negative connection. When you love yourself enough, you're free to let go of the victimization and fear. This also frees you to move forward in your life and gives you a brand-new perspective. Coding forgiveness takes the power away from the transgressor and gives it back to you.

Melany had been waiting for this freedom all her life. She hadn't realized that she had remained attached even after she chose not to see those family members anymore.

But her new code of forgiveness reframed her relationship with them and with herself. She finally found the freedom she'd been longing for.

Moving Toward Love

Longing can be another form of severe attachment. In cases of unrequited or lost love, you could be steeped in longing and desperate attachment, an energy that continues to keep you isolated and alone.

If you find yourself attached in this way, it will be very important to decode longing and code the ability to let go. Your attachment to an old, lost love energetically binds you to that person, sending clear signals to the Universe that no new love is needed because you're already connected. That connection may be totally one-sided or limited and dishonoring, but because of your longing, it's likely to be all you get.

And if you're dealing with old offenses, try coding forgiveness for others and yourself. It may be surprising, but when you let go of the attachment, you're finally free to connect in a genuine and healthy way.

Any division between you and others (even division through overattachment) belongs to the ego. In fact, codes of inadequacy, unworthiness, fear, and envy are all measuring devices of the ego. In order to release these, you need to redefine yourself according to your invulnerable, truly valuable, and all-loving eternal spirit. This definition needs to be held at a very real and experiential level and not merely in the mind. It needs to gently vibrate in your emotional resonance, the loving core of your life-force energy. So code the ability to feel this wonderful connection.

Meditate on your own heart center and open up to the life-changing power and truth within.

You can choose to code an awareness of this abiding peace whenever you meet with any kind of divisive experience—or when anything causes feelings of envy or discontent. Code love and peace; then drop your consciousness into your heart center. Give yourself over to that tranquil, nonstriving feeling. Living from your heart releases conflict and allows you to find present peace, one of the greatest codes you can achieve.

Taking the time to stop and connect with your own eternal heart is an important part of the Universal force of love. This is where the consciousness of Divine light resides, and when you connect with that, you find the real source of love in all its forms. This vital force is a powerful energy sparked by the breath of eternity. It starts with your own soul and constantly generates abounding love—for you, for your life, for the world, and for all the other souls that share it.

Remember, the vortex of this beautiful vibration starts within. Meditate on the force of love growing in your own heart center, and never forget this truth: Choosing value for yourself is one of your soul's greatest desires. When you live in this new, healthy, and harmonious code of self-love, you will have the unlimited power of Universal love at your disposal.

CHAPTER 14

THE BREAKTHROUGH FORCE OF JOY

"Surely joy is the condition of life."

— **Henry David Thoreau**

It's easy to see how Spirit and love are natural, activating forces in the Universe. Spirit connects, assists, and inspires; and we are all one with the heart of this creative force. Love is an extension and expression of that. It's a river of energy that moves through the Universe with powerful but tender intention.

But what about joy? Is it, indeed, a natural condition of life as Thoreau's words indicate? Many people are so miserable, or perhaps even just bored enough to think that joy is far from the natural state of humanity. Yet this, too, is an energetic force that—like Spirit and love—has a far-reaching influence in both your personal experience and in the world itself. Driven by elements such as desire and excitement, joy is both motivation and outcome in life. It's a present current, the river of which is always available; and we have the option to step into the sweet flow of happiness at any time. So why does it feel so elusive?

Although many people would say their lives are far from happy, they find that all they do is driven by the desire for joy. We work to make the money we think will bring us the things that will make us happy. We seek romance out of the desire for love and bliss. We go on vacations to experience delightful getaways. As a result, we often see happiness as a special—and for some reason rare—occurrence. But we can engage in joyous emotions in even the most mundane situations, if we choose.

Joy to You and Me

When joy expands, it showers the world with a highly charged energy that brings light to all who share it. This generates a lot of creative action, and as people who live with a joyful attitude can tell you, it generates a lot of magnetic attraction as well. For this and so many reasons, it is a noble and endlessly beneficial pursuit to ignite this wildly expansive force in your life.

Igniting Enthusiasm

The first ignitor of this powerful current is *enthusiasm*. Unfortunately, this incredibly strong energy is so easily derailed. Without any enthusiasm, your life force seeps away, and you find that you're dragging yourself through your day. When that happens, your misery can make it difficult to live in alignment with Universal flow. In essence, a joyless life makes it impossible to attract and receive. Your life force pools around you with dark and dense energy that resists the flow of happiness to come. So clearly, it's important to *consciously* create—and code—some enthusiasm for your life, for your goals, and for your everyday experiences.

Enthusiasm combines the energy of excitement in the present and optimism about the future. It calls you to be glad about what you've got going on now as well as looking expectantly to the future. When you maintain this as an ongoing approach, it lightens your vibration so much that it can accelerate and propel your intentions into rapid completion and fruition.

To generate enthusiasm, your positive outlook needs to be an undercurrent to the movement of your life. That's why the coding process can be so very helpful. You can consistently code the ability to create happiness and to trust your own resourcefulness. Code joy for today and optimism for the future. Then remember to support these codes in the mundane choices of your daily life. Create as many little moments of joy as you can, see the value of all the happy experiences around you, and be grateful.

Igniting Appreciation

The next ignitor of joy is a consciousness of gratitude. Our never-ending thoughts are often random. Some deny value, and some conclusions consciously acknowledge it. Unfortunately, we often fall into reactive patterns where we examine everything that's wrong with barely a nod to what's right or good.

Real appreciation acknowledges the value in yourself, your relationships, your career experiences, the things you own, and your life in general. When you have heartfelt gratitude in your daily life, it brings an ongoing flow of joy. But without gratitude in the present, the code of hopelessness makes it difficult to forge optimism for the future.

Appreciation can and should be coded, but it also needs to be consciously chosen and practiced. For those who are unhappy, this may seem like an unusual and difficult task, but creating this one code may be all you need to rid yourself of the unhappiness you feel. In fact, conscious appreciation and self-love are two of the most joyous and highly charged, positively magnetic vibrations. When you combine the attitudes of appreciation and enthusiasm, you engender the *emotion of excitement,* another component that ignites the force of joy.

Igniting Excitement

Life is an adventure that brings new potential every single day. Yet how often do you feel excited? People often reserve their excitement for big events and special occasions, but it can actually be a joyous way of life. You do have the option to get excited about the little things—as well as the big things—and maintain the emotional intention of that throughout your day. And if you code the habit of *looking* for things to get excited about, you will start to find more and more.

It has taken me a while to cultivate this habit, but now getting excited over the silly little things has become a big part of my life. In fact, it's a lot of fun! Flowers excite me. Music excites me. When I see a bird or a chipmunk, it makes me smile. And when I notice flowering bushes or trees as I'm driving down the road, I feel like the Universe is giving me a bouquet.

The irony of life is that we often dismiss the importance of what's already incredibly valuable because we're too busy striving to create value somewhere else. Over time we take these wonderful things so much for granted that we don't even notice them at all. We have to *choose* to see the miraculous and re-ignite the real excitement we've lost in our constant striving to make life more exciting.

Coding Points

It's time to bring more joy to your life. Use the following statements in your coding process to expand the ignitors of enthusiasm, appreciation, and excitement and to bring more joy to your life every day. Use your coding journal to record your experience and any additional statements you'd like to use.

Decoding:
> *I decode the habit of being blasé and indifferent.*
> *I decode patterns of being too busy to enjoy and appreciate my life.*
> *I decode unhappiness.*
> *I decode boredom.*

Coding:
> *I code the ability to acknowledge all that I have to value now.*
> *I code the ability to see myself and my life as a miracle.*
> *I code enthusiasm and fun now, and optimism for the future.*
> *I code joy, peace, belief, and bliss.*
> *I code smiles.*
> *I code the ability to be happy every day.*
> *I code a joyful outlook now and always.*

In addition to getting excited about the little things, you also need to maintain enthusiasm about your goals—and not just the end results of your goals, but about your process, too. In fact, seek out anything that could bring you excitement, and enjoy!

You *are* a miracle, and your life is a miracle, too. When you get excited about yourself and your experience, it ignites the joy generator in the Universe.

Breaking Through the Boredom

The first reactive pattern that blocks the force of joy is boredom or monotony. This lackluster energy is quite common, even for busy people who are always on the run. If you're engaged in the same activities over and over, that repetition and sameness can build a sluggish life-force momentum, which causes you to be dull and your results to be slow in coming.

If this sounds like you, you'll have to shake things up a bit. Increase your optimism and boost your energy by maintaining a clear and ongoing intention to keep your life interesting. This creates an attitude of excitement no matter what is (or is *not*) going on.

A lot of us don't think there's anything remarkable happening unless we're scheduling our next big trip or planning our next remodel, but that doesn't have to be our truth. We can make things interesting every single day. Code a clear perception of the quality of your life, and decode your attitudes of boredom and tedium. Mix up your routine. Do something different and choose to have some fun each day. Let yourself become interested in your life again.

Lighten Up!

Another reactive pattern blocking joy and enthusiasm is feeling burdened. This is a difficult yet common reaction. For some it comes from the logistical struggle of having too many tasks, while for others it's the emotional stress of too much responsibility. Both challenges can seem never ending and totally overwhelming.

We need to reduce our excessive task orientation and balance our life-force energy by adding pleasant activities into the mix. We also need to *release* the need to solve everything—and have every answer—immediately.

Decode urgency, stress, and striving. Adjust your perception to consider the value that each task brings to your life, and choose to project some joy into it. Lighten the vibration. Bring it to a higher level, and let yourself create a new pattern of joy and relaxation no matter what's going on.

Don't just drag your way through life; *dance* your way through it! Find joy in all that you do, and affirm that every single day is a blessing. Know that every task and choice is your own life expressing itself. See the power and the purpose in that, and recognize joy as an ever-present adjacent possibility.

Down and Depressed

Perhaps the most difficult reactive pattern blocking your force of joy is depression. Sometimes depression can be situational, an emotional response to the difficult circumstances you find yourself in. A feeling of hopelessness can arise in traumatic or deeply sad situations. Yet some depression is more pervasive. It transcends events and becomes more chronic, weaving unhappiness throughout your life. Either way, depression is definitely a full body-mind experience, and it can be debilitating.

Depression can be the "natural condition" for some people. In fact, chronic depression is often called *anhedonia,* the inability to be happy. It may seem irreversible, but no matter how deeply entrenched you are in this reactive pattern, you can decode the habit and code the ability to be truly happy.

Let yourself get professional help. Vent your feelings and code the ability to respond in your own highest interest, slowly reestablishing a greater sense of your own power and value. Little by little, you can bring a brighter emotional vibration to things. As you decode depression, you will free yourself from the old, stuck, unhappy energy. And as you code peace, self-empowerment, and enthusiasm for your own life, you will find yourself awakening more and more genuine feelings of joy.

Wrangling the Worry

Excessive worry is another reactive pattern that blocks your ability to live in peace and happiness. The energy of enthusiasm by its nature is sourced in optimistic interpretation, so let yourself decode worry and negation at every opportunity. To reclaim your joy, you must first notice your worry patterns. Do a releasing affirmation, such as *I have the ability to change my response. I always have the power to let go of worry.* Decode your attachment to this habit, and code the choice to live in peace, power, hope, and joy instead.

Coding Points

Use the following statements during the coding technique to release your blocks to this powerful force of joy, and track your progress in your coding journal. Ignite the excitement and enthusiasm you deserve to have about your life every day.

Decoding:

I decode boredom and dissatisfaction.
I decode the habit of dismissing my life.
I decode the habit of seeing my life as a burden.
I decode worry and unhappiness.
I decode resentment of my life.
I decode habits of depression and fear.

Coding:

I code happiness and feelings of joy.
I code responses of peace and trust.
I code gratitude for all I have and all I am.
I code the ability to find peace and joy in any moment.
I code interest in myself and my life.
I code habits of fun and enjoyment.
I code the freedom to be happy any time.

Karen's Story, in Her Own Words

A client named Karen had unknowingly lost the joy in her life. It took a while, but over time she had established a dull routine of just getting by. She was emotionally empty, and she finally reached a point where she wanted that to change. Here's what she told me:

I hadn't realized how much of a rut I was in. My life was the same old routine over and over and over again. Not only that, there was hardly anything I found myself looking forward to. It was just the same old drab stuff—not life, just existence.

I guess a lot of people don't expect much happiness, and that's exactly what happened to me. Depending on the day, my life was either dull or hard, and there wasn't anything that I could—or even wanted to—do differently. A friend said that I was suffering from undiagnosed depression, but other than the fact that I just couldn't see anything worthwhile, I really didn't have anything to be depressed about!

When I learned the decoding and coding technique, it was so easy and took so little time that I figured I might as well try it. I even thought that maybe I could return to being the happy and carefree girl I had been in my 20s! To be honest, that girl seemed so different from my present self that I really didn't think it was going to be possible. But I tried anyway.

Every morning I decoded depression and unhappiness. I decoded stress and boredom, too. Then I coded the ability to see my life as fun and exciting. I coded enthusiasm for my job and even a greater love and appreciation for my kids. I did lots of coding throughout the day—a few moments here or there, whenever I noticed myself starting to drag or feel down.

It took a while, but eventually I started to notice myself smiling more, and others noticed my mood change, too. More people sought me out, I guess because I was more fun to be with. I was just enjoying things more than I had in years. I had a spring in my step and a smile for the day.

Things are really different now. Being with my kids is fun again. Even doing housework is fun! And when times get hard, or I fall into my old patterns, I know that I can just let that be okay and recode my view of things. It's funny, where before I never found things to be happy about—or to look forward to—now I find all sorts of things to enjoy. My life is lighter, and I feel lighter, too. My family is closer, doing more together and having more fun. People say I'm like a different person, but I'm really the same—the same happy person I was 20 years ago. That girl has come back to me!

Out of the Dark

Many people are more depressed than they realize, just going along with their schedule with very little happiness in their hearts. This seems to get worse as we get older, but it's not restricted to age. No matter how old we are or what the situation is, it's time to *choose* a joyous perception, to code smiles and happiness and the priority of having fun.

Your spirit came here to enjoy life, and you don't have to be planning something special to experience that. Stop. Appreciate. Enjoy the little things—the sweet desserts, the loving smiles, your favorite music. Code each of these moments with joy, and your blessings and bliss will expand.

CHAPTER 15

THE BREAKTHROUGH FORCE OF ACTION

"And the day came when the risk to remain tight in a bud was more painful than the risk it took to blossom."

— attributed to Anaïs Nin

The word *action* implies motion; it assumes intention—and direction. You can feel the energy in the word itself, and you can sense the power of this breakthrough force whenever you awaken it in your life.

Most people think that taking action means only focusing on their goals. But there are lots of different types of action that they never consider. Each one is equally important to your sense of happiness and your potential results. And every single type of action can be coded.

You may have to code the ability to take risks in order to set yourself on this path. Many people feel that it's the action that's risky, but that's not nearly so frightening as *not* acting in your own behalf. Staying in the status quo may lull you into a state of comfort and inactivity, but it also pretty much guarantees your life will stay the same as well.

Coding is a safe and peaceful activity that you can apply to anything you do.

Any action you take is inextricably connected to the next breakthrough force of responsibility, so you will find that these two chapters complement each other in some important ways. Clearly it is necessary to be responsible for your life so that you can take the action you need to move forward. For these forces to shine forth, you must become much more conscious of your options in the present and prioritize your choices according to your own truth.

Igniting Consciousness

Remember this: Action is conscious. *Reaction* is usually not, and most of our lives are spent in the state of reaction. Consciousness, the art of living in an awakened state, is the first ignitor of action. This includes *all* the options we have in our daily life—behavioral, cognitive, practical, logistical, and energetic. When we are conscious, we can take action in each of these.

We sail through life, riding the current of necessity, often unaware of the myriad options we have. The problem is that this unconscious living results in unconscious creation. Becoming conscious calls for us to look at our life and say, *I'm free to take action in any way that honors me, in any way I choose. Every action is a choice that brings a consequence to me and my life.*

After all, why are we doing all this? Surely there is a deeper purpose than paying the rent. Our souls long for us to take a clearer look at life, to become conscious, and to choose to take higher actions that lead to self-mastery and greater recognition of our true value. Our worthiness requires conscious, purposeful action, so throughout the day, stop and take stock. You may find it helpful to write in or review your coding journal to focus your awareness. Code a clearer understanding of things, and when you see your next move, make it a priority to take action.

Igniting True Priorities

Higher action also requires discipline. Rather than looking at this as self-sacrifice, your choice of discipline really means deciding what your priorities are—and taking action in that direction. Then choose to create an emotional and habitual momentum that supports that.

What *are* your priorities? Code the wisdom to know what's in your highest and best interest; then code the courage to live with focused and purposeful action. If achieving a certain goal is most important, you may need to set aside the time to take the steps to work on it. For example, if your goal is losing weight, then you know the necessary conscious action is to eat less and exercise more. These and other actions of priority take discipline and courage, but not only can you code the active habits themselves, you can also code the *courage* and the *discipline* you need. In fact, coding is another form of action you can take in any pursuit at all.

So many people don't prioritize themselves or their goals. Many put their own dreams on the back burner so consistently that they aren't aware of what's really important to them. Still others don't even know what they prefer in life—nor do they realize that they're allowed to have a preference! If you're in this group, you need to decode this pattern of self-dismissal. If you don't, your life is going to stay on the back burner, and your energy is going to be dense and unmoving because your action is always taken on other people's behalf. It's time to give your life back to yourself! Decode old patterns of passive inaction, and code conscious self-priority instead.

Igniting Presence

Action is a powerful breakthrough force, but you must bring your consciousness to the *present* in order to activate it. You can't take action in the past, and although you can plan the future, you can't guarantee what you'll do when the time comes.

But presence gives you the power to change your energy now, to code new patterns and shift your emotions immediately. These are all important actions that actually change the quality of your life, although they're often not considered actions at all. Never forget, there's an energetic action that takes place every moment, whether we choose to consciously direct it or not.

The present is the only potential time to act, so you need to ask yourself, *What can I do now? What can I change now? How can I use this moment to enhance the quality of my life—to direct the emotional experience I'm having?* Code a willingness to act on your thoughts and behaviors. Code consciousness and strength in every present moment, and you can—and will—change everything.

Coding Points

Use the following statements during your coding process to help ignite presence, priority, and consciousness in your life—and get your train of action back on track.

Coding:

I code greater awareness of the opportunities in my life.
I code consciousness in my choices and decisions.
I code self-priority.
I code discipline and strength.
I code the ability to take risks and act on my own behalf.
I code present action.
I code self-direction.
I code action in my thoughts.
I code the courage to take right action always.

Pro-Active or No-Active?

There are many hidden codes that continually stop us from taking action—and they can be enormous blocks to our happiness and our life's desires. These reactive patterns are often deeply indoctrinated, causing us to miss important opportunities to ignite our own action and finally break through. One of the most debilitating of these is hopelessness.

This dense, dark emotional pattern causes a paralysis of will and action. Hopelessness is deeply rooted in the expectation that any action would be fruitless, so why bother? This is often connected to patterns of powerlessness, an inner perception of weakness and ineffectuality. If you have thoughts like these, make sure you decode old misinformation about your lack of strength. Code inner power and the ability to express that in the world, no matter what issue you may feel hopeless about.

Don't let your action get stuck in a defeated attitude. No matter what's going on, open up your heart and life to the powerful force of hopeful action. Decode fearful assumptions and code an optimistic outlook instead. Remember, it's your responsibility to create your own code of hopeful expectation, and you can do it!

Not-So-Great Escapes!

It's a natural human tendency to want to get away from pain, unhappiness, anger, or any difficult emotion. Patterns of escapism are deeply rooted and repeated habits that we pursue in order to distract ourselves from discomfort—or even from some emotional experiences that don't seem so bad, such as boredom. Chronic escapism can wield quite a lot of power, whether it takes the form of ongoing distractions or debilitating addictions. These habits can include things such as too much TV, Internet gaming, overeating, smoking, or excessive drinking. The list is virtually endless, and most people do some sort of unhealthy avoidance almost every day. You know when you have these kinds of habits—and when you're using them to escape.

People tend to overeat or drink when they're angry, or even when they're just tired or bored. They also do so when they're hurt and feel the need to stuff down their feelings. This is an escapist reaction, but none of us have to live in this false code of distraction any longer.

The problem with addictions, and even numbing distractions, is that they keep us from achieving our goals—and from feeling happy. Every addiction feels good at the beginning because it gives us a false sense of support and comfort, allowing us to escape our true emotions. Eventually, however, all addictions become toxic, creating even more reactive patterns and deeper codes than the ones we're already trying to escape.

A little bit of distraction is fine. We may need some time to decompress from the stress of the day. But our action gets derailed when our escapist energies are entwined in much of our daily lives. Unhealthy habits wrap our intentions in unhappiness. Old distractions immobilize us and keep us stuck in the very patterns we grow to hate ourselves for. What a web of self-sabotage that weaves!

So when you're preparing to decode any of these unhealthy habits, make sure you look honestly at your behaviors and patterns. Record your observations and coding statements in your coding journal. Addictions can be some of the hardest areas to change, so let yourself take all the action you need, including getting professional help. Decode and release any pattern of escapism little by little, choice by choice, day by day. Remember to code the power to stay centered, focused, and in control. Make sure you decode the habit as well as the emotions behind it. In that way, you can release the pattern along with its source. Code healthy new habits; new actions; and peaceful, self-empowered behaviors. And remember, *every present moment is a fresh opportunity—and you always have the power to choose something new, no matter what you were doing just a moment ago!*

What's the Scatter?

Fragmented and scattered energy is a common resonant pattern that comes from too much emotion, multitasking, urgency, or distraction. Your focus, your life, and your energy are in pieces all around you because whatever's going on, it's just too much!

This abrasive vibration makes you feel on edge, off balance, or often dissatisfied. In order to create real happiness and quality of life, it definitely needs to be decoded. Such fragmented energy blocks your action and all too easily gets you off track.

For example, it's not uncommon to have so many mundane tasks that you become far too busy to take any real action in your own behalf. You can't take that bubble bath because you have to do the laundry. You can't work on your goal because you have to get dinner ready. But these aren't the actions that are really calling to you. Your inner desire is being dismissed while your outer demands are going in a dozen different directions.

Fragmented energy can also be sourced in self-doubt. Not believing in yourself splits your energy because you're looking for approval, valuing others' opinions more than your own, and always wondering what to think and how to behave. In this way, your mind goes into hyperdrive, scattering your very sense of who you are and keeping you confused about what you want in your life, never really knowing what kind of action to take.

Another source of scattered energy can be too many interests or options. Part of you may long to be a musician, while another part is called to painting or writing. You may jump from one desire to another, unable to figure out which is your true path. If this is the case, it will be important to consider what's really motivating you in order to determine what pursuit resonates with you the most.

But whether your fragmentation is from multiple longings, self-doubt, or just being too busy, you don't have to find every possible source in order to reign it in. Decode patterns of scattered energy and code clear and calm choices instead. Meditate on centering your energy. Code peaceful, focused attention and the intention to take self-directed action in your life.

Remember to cut down on some of your obligations and start prioritizing yourself. Take some time to consider what really calls to your heart of hearts, and then follow that direction. Patiently and calmly take the action that will move all your inner and outer goals forward.

Coding Points

So many people go through their lives being extremely busy, yet never taking any real personal or self-honoring action. If this sounds like you, use the following statements to decode the blocks and spark the amazing force of action to help you experience fulfillment and happiness.

Decoding:

I decode hopelessness.

I decode lack of energy and focus.

I decode habits of taking on too much.

*I decode habits of getting distracted from my
    own priorities.*

*I decode the need to escape. I decode the feelings that
    make me long to escape.*

I decode habits of scattered energy.

Coding:

*I code personal power and the ability to stay present
    and calm.*

I code balance and inner peace.

I code freedom, purpose, and happiness.

I code energy and action.

*I code healthy habits, new actions, and self-honoring
    choices.*

I code the power to choose right action.

I code freedom.

I code balance.

I code control.

Thomas Smoke-Free—Finally!

The addiction of smoking can be difficult to break. As with drugs and alcohol, there are all sorts of chemical components that feed the reactive pattern and reinforce the code.

There are also many ways these types of habits block our happiness, our action, and our authentic freedom. For example, they divert our energy, reducing our stamina and our ability to put effort into our desired activities. And the chemicals of smoking can be agitating, creating less peace and comfort in our daily tasks and in the pursuit of our goals. Not only that, the activity is time-consuming and isolating, putting up an energetic wall between us and those we might connect with. That's a lot of blocks for a habit that usually starts with the simple desire to fit in with friends.

Of course, Thomas might not have thought about his code of smoking on all these levels, but one thing was sure—he wanted to quit! So he used the Quantum Breakthrough Code to quit smoking, release anxiety, and manage his cravings whenever they came up. In addition, he coded some wonderful new habits, including embracing freedom and taking in life fully. These and other intentions are revealed in his decoding and coding statements.

Decoding:

I decode the toxic habit of smoking.
I decode unhealthy cravings to smoke.
I decode powerlessness over tobacco.
I decode unthinking choices.
I decode reactive patterns of stress and anxiety.
I decode thoughts that aren't present.

I decode addiction and self-abuse.
I decode the need to smoke.

Coding:
I code healthy habits for my body and well-being.
I code peace in the present moment.
I code power over smoking and tobacco.
I code the willingness to take life in fully.
I code freedom.
I code breath.
I code awareness of my spirit.

Thomas was finally able to quit smoking, and needless to say, this was a huge achievement! His old code of escapism might have felt hard to break through before, but he was able to completely decode it and open the way for his own genuine life force to flow freely. There were a few times when the longing returned, but Thomas told me they were easy to dismiss with a few quick coding techniques. He took action in a new direction, and the result was freedom, confidence, and personal power—the energies of which will expand throughout many areas of his life.

What habit would you like to free yourself from? What takes you off your path and stops you from pursuing the purposeful, self-honoring action that will bring greater joy and fulfillment to your life? It may not involve a physical pattern like Thomas had to deal with, but whatever it is, you *do* have the power to break through. And as Thomas experienced, the action you take will bring a truly exciting freedom where you know that all things *are* possible!

CHAPTER 16

THE BREAKTHROUGH FORCE OF RESPONSIBILITY

"You must take responsibility. You may not change the circumstances, the seasons, or the wind, but you can change yourself. That is something you have charge of."

— Jim Rohn

We each have the ability to engage in all the energies of happiness and success, and when we do, they become real forces in our lives. The final but most fundamental breakthrough force that we'll be discussing is *responsibility*. Those who live by the code of personal responsibility possess a high consciousness of their power, both in their lives and in the world, and this attitude lays the groundwork for real change.

The driving intention here is *owning* the emotional quality of your life. This means reviewing your options and considering the consequences of your actions. It's really the choice to be consciously self-directed and self-empowered, which is one of the most important choices you can make.

Most people *believe* they're taking responsibility for their lives, but have no idea how often they give this power away. They allow others to direct many of their choices—either out of fear, the need to please, or just a passive approach to things. But this is a code of submission, creating a nagging sense of emptiness as well as unsatisfying results.

On the other side of the coin, your self-responsible choices will result in feelings of fulfillment and experiences that bring you joy and self-honoring. Real self-direction comes from your inner awareness of your worth, a truth that will always bring greater happiness and more resplendent acknowledgment from the Universe.

It's important to note, however, that taking responsibility does not mean faulting yourself, whether for present problems or perceived past "misdeeds." Blame and responsibility are two very different things, and that difference is energetically significant. Blaming yourself finds you faulty and devalues you in your own estimation. *Responsibility is the choice to take charge of how you want to live from this moment forward.* It's in the present that we direct our future.

You can learn from the past and evaluate what you want to do differently from here on out. Take charge of the present and every moment forward, but remember to be gentle with yourself. If you miss a beat, fall into old patterns, or make some unhealthy choices, you can always adjust and move on. In fact, real responsibility requires this conscious, loving, and flexible approach every single day. Your coding journal will be especially helpful in this process, as you can review and renew your commitment to a new way of life.

It's clear that engaging in the other breakthrough forces means you're making responsible choices, but your focus can go even deeper. There are several things that you can do to ignite the directive force of responsibility as an undercurrent in your life. The elements of choice and consciousness will accelerate a deep sense of self-empowerment, bringing clarity and calm to your ongoing decisions, big and small.

Igniting Conscious Responses

You have an ever-present ability to choose a new and different response. This is your *response*-ability. And this—your ability to make truly considered responses—ignites self-actualization and present power.

Unaware reaction is the hallmark of a reactive pattern. Instead of spontaneously reacting, however, you always have the ability to stop and consider before doing anything. It is a conscious choice to respond to events, emotions, people, and situations—everything in your life—in a more deliberate way. The fact is, whether you realize it or not, you have the right and the power to choose how you want to respond in any given moment.

The problem with most of us is that we just react, hence the term *reactive patterns.* When in a negative reactive pattern, we're not taking responsibility and not tapping our full power or potential. Persisting at our gut level, spontaneous reactions set up some negative codes in certain situations or with certain types of people—and our patterns just repeat and repeat.

Whatever situation we may find ourselves in, we need to stop and consciously think about how we *want* to respond, and then we can code that healthy habit. We must remind ourselves of our power—and consider the consequences of allowing ourselves to keep on living in our reactive patterns. Remember the soul's directive to act in an authentic and self-honoring way. *That* is the height of responsibility.

Igniting Self-Honoring

The full force of responsibility is ignited by conscious self-honoring and self-actualization. This is the decision to take responsibility for your physical well-being and your behavioral habits—as well as the very real energetic consequences of the choices you make all the time.

What is conscious self-actualization? It's acting with awareness and authenticity, releasing habits of escapism and old patterns of following the path of least resistance. It's knowing that you can redirect your daily habits in purposeful and healthy ways, ones that honor your priorities and acknowledge your value. Whether you're making a big decision or seemingly small choices in your daily habits of eating, drinking, or figuring out how you'll spend your time, you simply don't have to react in the same old ways. Intervene by saying, *I am not living in my old reactive patterns anymore!* Then stop to consider all your options.

The truth is, you face thousands of choices every day, and each one of them can be consciously self-directed. Code choices that honor you in your daily routines. And code self-awareness in all the decisions of your life.

I have to say that, in a lot of ways, the responsibility of being truly conscious and self-actualized was taught to me by Louise Hay—by reading her books, by understanding the choices she has made, and also by having the great good fortune of spending time with her. She is a strong proponent of doing what you want to do, what you prefer, and what honors you. And if anyone has a statement against that, she shuts it down, always defending a person's right to make his or her own choices.

I remember a phone call I had with Louise one day in April. She lives in California, and she had just come in from gardening. I told her that I was looking at four inches of snow. She proceeded to tell me that was *my choice.* I was 40 years old, and I have to tell you, I had never, ever considered leaving my hometown to go to a different climate. It had never even occurred to me to ask myself if I would like to move or where I would like to live, and never had I considered that I could choose a different region or even another country!

It was only after that comment from Louise that I decided to investigate why I was still living in Ohio and what was making me stay. I guess I wanted to be near my family, but it was so revealing that I had never even thought about any other option before. I had accepted other people's expectations without any conscious awareness of it! In truth, I had unknowingly developed a reactive pattern of obligation and unconscious self-dismissal, willingly limiting my own options.

The lesson is to *live* in the force of responsibility, to be self-actualized and honoring in your everyday habits, and to stop and consider your own heart's desire in your important (although sometimes seemingly automatic) choices. Remember, when you consistently actualize yourself and your life, your energy of responsibility will mean *no regrets.*

Igniting Your Emotional Power

The third ignitor of responsibility is *emotional self-empowerment,* the choice to consistently take responsibility for the *emotional* quality of your daily life. The reality is, only *you* have the power to direct how you feel.

Although we'd like to pin this on others, no one else can be responsible for the feelings we experience throughout the day. Of course, there are many people who influence our ups and downs. Critical or negative individuals are likely to create uncomfortable emotions; those who are hostile may evoke fear. However, it's up to us to choose if we want to linger in those feelings. We can react like a pinball, being pushed around like an inanimate object; or we can take charge and take action, hitting that negativity out of the park. We can become conscious and responsible for creating the happiness we seek.

This is a huge life lesson and a driving imperative: We can ignite our own *emotional* enlightenment. We can live in joy instead of disinterest, peace instead of anger, and trust instead of fear. We are free to choose, to vent how we feel, and then to decide what we want to do about the emotions and the situations we find ourselves in. It's a real option to decode the unwanted emotional patterns—and to code strong personal reactions of self-care along with the peaceful or happy feelings we want to live in.

It's important to be flexible and forgiving of yourself, though, for some emotions are spontaneous and extremely strong. You may have to deal with those harsh issues over and over, venting your feelings and maybe even getting help if needed. But keep in mind that you always have the ability to redirect your focus away from your negative conclusions and code peace, trust, and self-love instead.

This is your ongoing emotional choice. It's not really the big moments that define you; it's the accumulation of all your little moments that truly and energetically make you who you are. And if you aren't willing to take responsibility for the happiness of all your finer moments, then you won't be able or willing to take responsibility for the full experience of happiness in the major areas of your life.

This is one of the biggest powers that coding can bring to you. Engaging in emotional responsibility allows you to determine your emotional response and the vibrational projection of your predominant feelings. And when you code ongoing options of higher emotions and more peaceful feelings, you're given the opportunity to shift outer events and relationships to reflect these profound inner changes. The power of a genuinely happy and self-directed consciousness attracts people who want to enhance your life just as you do, and it brings situations that vibrate with the same resonance of your inner joy.

Coding Points

To make considered responses a new way of life, use the following statements while engaging in the coding process. Whether physically, cognitively, or emotionally, you can redefine any situation, any person, and any reaction. Code choices that honor you. And don't forget to code a higher emotional quality to your life as well. If self-priority is a problem for you—as it is for millions of others—keep the following coding statements in mind.

Decoding:

I decode old patterns of unconscious choices.
I decode unthinking reactions.
I decode habits of negating and marginalizing myself.
I decode anxiety and fear of taking risks.
I decode self-dismissal.

Coding:

I code a deeper awareness of all my choices throughout the day.

I code calm and considered responses.

I code power over every decision.

I code freedom from responsibility for others.

I code responsibility for myself.

I code self-priority.

I code comfort and peace in prioritizing myself.

I code joyous self-awareness. The choices I make honor me.

I code self-love and real self-care.

I code peace and comfort in all I do.

I code happiness and a new point of view.

I code freedom of response. I am free to enjoy my life.

I code the ability to experience joy in the little things.

I code a joyous attitude and smile.

Freeing the Victim

The force of responsibility is like the flame in a forge, and the power of self-direction can forge an irresistible life force. While there are many common reactive patterns that can block this dynamic force, one of the most significant blocks is *victimization*. Remember, these negative patterns are themselves compelling codes. And although they may be hidden deep within, they are real influences in our lives nonetheless. The block of victimization is a pervasive, yet often unspoken, attitude toward life where we essentially just give our power away.

This attitude may be rooted in a difficult past, originating at a time when others could easily take our power away. As time goes on, this experience can expand into a more global perception, and we become convinced that other people *still* have more power in our present life. That assumption makes us passive, a code that acts as even more evidence of our victimhood. As a result, we also believe that we are not capable of taking our power back. This paralyzes us with inaction and makes personal responsibility impossible due to the false belief that there is simply nothing we can do about our circumstances. This is an important issue, so let yourself be honest about how much power you give to others by letting yourself feel like a victim. You may be surprised by what you find.

I once found myself feeling hurt and angry because of someone's unfeeling dismissal. I couldn't seem to let it go. I just kept brooding and feeling upset. Eventually, I realized that I was unknowingly giving my emotional power away and letting myself feel victimized. My anger was only attaching me to that experience and perpetuating the emotions!

So I decoded any attachment to that person and coded freedom and happiness instead. It had been bugging me for weeks, but it wasn't until I did the decoding and coding positions that I realized how totally trapped I had become by my own negative reaction. Within minutes of completing the process, however, I was laughing at the folly of letting that person turn so many of my happy hours into misery! But I finally was able to let go of it all and was feeling genuinely happy and free. From then on, whenever any thought of that individual came up, I spent just a few moments doing the same thing—and getting the same happy emotional results. I had taken responsibility for my emotional experience and turned my feelings completely around. That was the goal. And interestingly enough, that person has actually been kinder to me ever since!

Passive and Powerless

People often become very accustomed to being powerless in their lives. They do what they *have* to do without any regard to what they *want* to do. They fulfill others' expectations more willingly than their own. They allow themselves to be criticized, mistreated, or dismissed without making any attempt to limit or change that. And if they do try to change, they usually give up at the first sign of resistance.

This is a passive and disempowered approach to life. To many people, there's a certain kind of comfort in not having to take charge. After all, it seems like it's the easiest way to go—the path of least resistance and no responsibility. Not taking responsibility means never being "wrong." It means less effort and less risk—or at least that's how it seems.

But this interpretation is entirely false. It actually creates more unease, and it takes a lot more effort to constantly carry the misery that goes with this passive approach. It's also a far bigger risk because living with an undercurrent of powerlessness makes you lose all sense of hope. And you simply can't feel genuinely happy without power in the present and hope for the future.

Your soul longs for you to remember the absolute truth: *You are a powerful force in the world.* No matter what you've been through in the past, no matter how often or how long you've given your power away, you *do* have the ability to take your power back. Code the ability to say no, to demand respect, and to take action. And code new patterns of making conscious choices that empower you. In fact, it's your *responsibility* to do so.

Insecurity Blanket!

This pattern of giving away power can layer on feelings of fear that are woven with beliefs of insecurity. First, you're unsure of yourself. Then you become unsure of the world, filled with uncertainty—whether it's financial, personal, or even physical. And it's not uncommon for emotional insecurities to manifest in relationship problems and chronic unease.

This pervasive fear makes you think that you don't have the resourcefulness to handle the vagaries of life. It also engenders resistance and isolation. Why isolation? Because when you view the world as unsafe, your natural reaction will be to retreat and stay out of it. It's a fear-based choice that brings feelings of loneliness and unhappiness, cutting you off from connection even more.

Unfortunately, you're not just isolating yourself emotionally and socially, but energetically as well. This kind of disempowerment takes you out of the flow of synchronicity, removing you from the current of energy that connects you with people and solutions in a harmonious way.

Mary's Misery

One of the most common codes of insecurity manifests in a driving need for approval. This longing for acceptance often comes as a result of uncaring or dismissive parents. Such was the case for one young woman named Mary, whose father was abusively critical.

When we investigated her need for approval, we found that it had expanded far beyond her father to virtually everyone in her life. Yet when she examined her situation according to her soul truth, she was able to view her father as someone who was desperate for power and seeking to grasp it from a helpless and trusting child. She changed her old code and was finally able to define her dad in an entirely different way, and as a result, she was able to code a new and liberated response to him and to her world.

She was amazed that he no longer had any power over her, and she now saw this as an opportunity to change her response to everyone around her, decoding the striving that had become a way of life. She coded equality and gave herself permission not to need anyone's approval. She was finally comfortable and relieved to let go of the longing that had kept her unhappy for so long. This is what *response*-ability is all about—shifting your perception; reclaiming your power; and coding a new, healthy pattern of responses.

Coding Points

If feelings of insecurity, victimization, or just being too passive are an issue for you, make sure you put these patterns on the list of things you want to decode. Write them down in your coding journal to make sure they don't fall by the wayside. Responsibility is an important piece of the energetic puzzle because it deeply influences all the other breakthrough forces. In fact, you'll find that a lot of these negative codes are layered and connected. The network of habits and beliefs tie you up, blocking your energy centers and your intentions. So let yourself code comfort and resourcefulness. Bring your emotional power back, and use these coding statements to shift your responses. When your response to life changes, your life changes as well.

Decoding:

I decode insecurity and fear.

I decode patterns of being too passive.

I decode patterns of self-doubt.

I decode any old patterns of giving my power away.

I decode patterns of victimization, even the ones I'm not aware of.

I decode attachment to others and what they think.

Coding:

I code the knowledge that I am resourceful.

I code the ability to take charge, and I choose to do so at every opportunity.

I code freedom and happiness in and of myself.

I code power and peace in any situation.

I code a take-charge attitude toward my life.

I code the comfort and freedom I need to put myself first.

I code strength and happiness now and always.

To charge your life with the breakthrough force of responsibility, it will be necessary to start taking your power back. Use the technique to decode your patterns that make you feel passive and powerless. Code a new point of view, one where you are front and center and taking responsibility for how you want your life to go. In addition to using the coding technique, follow these guidelines as you go about your daily routines:

- Be conscious that you have the option to reclaim your power in your choices, your behaviors, and in all the ways you live your life.

- Respond with self-awareness. Ask what you can do differently, healthfully, and powerfully.

- Take more action on your own behalf.

- Set boundaries with others, and prioritize yourself.

- Affirm: *I know that only I have the power to direct my life. I claim my power now and always.*

You no longer need to remain powerless, insecure, or victimized in any way. All these reactive patterns can be broken through. You can decode your fearful and limiting responses and recode a healthier, more empowered approach. Even if these old patterns have guided your life and seem to be a part of your very nature, they can still be changed.

Responsibility is the key, and turning that key means the difference between staying stuck in doubt and resistance or moving forward with purpose and joy. So get ready to energize your life like never before. As you make the coding technique your own, the exhilarating power of the breakthrough forces will become your new nature—the new way you do life.

PART V

CODE TRIP

"If the doors of perception were cleansed,
everything would appear to man as it is, infinite."

— William Blake

CHAPTER 17

CODING A NEW WAY OF LIFE

*"Life isn't about finding yourself.
Life is about creating yourself."*

— **attributed to George Bernard Shaw**

Every day—every moment—your life is evolving, moving in one direction or another. Whether you realize it or not, you are always planting the seeds of tomorrow's harvest. Your choices today will determine if those seeds turn into beautiful blossoms and delicious fruit or prickly brambles and strangling weeds. In every present moment you have the option to make a different choice, and now you have an energetic tool to help you do so.

Sometimes I wonder why I was given the information about the Quantum Breakthrough Code. This book has been by far the most personal I've written, and in some ways the most exciting. It's so personal because of the way I received the information—a message from Spirit to be shared. This is also why it's so very thrilling, sparking unknown potential. Of course, on the other side of the excitement coin, you'll always find some risk. For those reasons, this book has also been the most difficult to write. It is filled with mystery, amazing wonder, and repeated questions.

I have found the coding process to be just that—a process. There are times when I haven't had the success I was looking for, like when I was trying to decode insomnia. I was so desperate to fall asleep that I became agitated and urgent and of course couldn't even relax, much less sleep. Yet there were other times when doing a simple coding totally reversed my mood—or immediately gave me stamina, energy, and excitement when I was feeling tired or unmotivated.

In fact, I would have to say that this coding technique has changed thousands of moments for me over the past couple of years. That is, I believe, how we change the nature of our lives: moment by moment, making clear and conscious choices and giving our energy a new direction. No longer do we have to just give in and settle for tedium or suffering as our main course. Instead, we can move forward with a new voice, a new vision, and a new way of life.

Coding Every Day

Although many people have told me that they experienced immediate emotional results with a big change in their lives over a matter of weeks, I have found that the key to the success of this process is doing it over and over again with many statements addressing a wide variety of issues. Repeat, repeat, repeat—and keep on repeating! We haven't created our complex network of fears, doubts, hesitations, addiction, and other reactive patterns overnight, so it may take a while to get rid of them. Your coding journal is an invaluable tool for recording your journey.

You may, on the other hand, be one of those people who quickly make radical changes, and you can use the coding to accelerate that which you want to achieve. Don't be discouraged if your intentions require a lot of focus and follow-through. Repetition is already a power in your life. That's why the reactive patterns can be so controlling—they just keep on coming. In fact, it's the power of unconscious repetition that keeps you stuck.

So what is the solution? If it's the power of repetition that unconsciously keeps you stuck, it's the conscious and pervasive coding that will get you unstuck. But this repetition doesn't have to be a burden. It can just be a few moments of intentional action taken several times a day. Make it a part of your life, just like affirmations, relaxation, and breathing!

Here are some tips that can help you do so:

- Repeat the decoding and coding at regular intervals, and do quick repetitions within different situations.

- Even if you have several reactive patterns that you want to decode, don't try to do it all at once. Pick just one thing, and repeat various statements for that specific issue.

- Code beneficial states like freedom, release, personal power, and peace by using smaller phrases and single words many times a day.

- Whether you're changing a mildly challenging state or working on an important issue such as fear or addiction, don't be desperate or urgent. Do it calmly and peacefully, without attachment to outcome.

- Have fun with the technique and code a playful attitude.

- Take your time. Let it be okay if you need to repeat your new codes for a while. Some codes, like happiness, need to become a part of you for the rest of your life.

Different people respond in different ways. Most notice a sense of peace, happiness, or even just release as an immediate result. Some have even bigger changes right away, especially when the issue is a temporary concern.

I was working on the phone with a woman who was in a very difficult economic cycle. She wanted to move to another state and apply for a job that she'd heard about. Unfortunately, she hadn't been able to sell her house or get an interview. After talking to her for a bit, it became clear that she had a deep fear of poverty, yet a strong expectation of it. I taught her how to decode those things, and I recommended that she decode desperation as well.

She then coded self-trust, peace of mind, patience, and calm determination. She could feel the wonderful energy of the experience as we engaged in these and a few more positive and optimistic codes. Before we finished, I suggested that she repeat the whole process two or three times each day in addition to doing several quick codes of happiness, trust, and peace. Two weeks later, I received a message from her saying that she had sold her home and had gotten an interview for the position she wanted. She told me she would be moving soon, but she was going to be a "coder" for the rest of her life.

That was an unusually rapid shift. Others, like Emma, who is working on weight loss, may have to invest more time. She has begun to lose quite a bit, but she's still working on it, and even if it takes several months, that's okay. The important thing is, she's sure changing her relationship with food. In fact, her approach to eating and to exercise is entirely different now.

Some people might resist doing the coding on a regular basis at first. But you can make it a recharging power that brings light and energy to every part of your life. It's such an ongoing influence that I urge you to consider it similar to eating and breathing and drinking water. We all do that every day, and many of us also exercise several times a week. Like all those things, coding is a healthy part of life. It's a part of what keeps us going. It is sustenance and renewal all at once, so let yourself release resistance and repeat it often with a happy, playful, and excited attitude.

Decoding Resistance

Some people feel a great deal of resistance to doing this process. It may be because they aren't ready to let go of what is familiar. No matter how unhealthy something is for us, it can still feel very comfortable—even if it's the exact opposite of what we need for a happy life.

There's something seductive about staying in our patterns. You may be desperate for change, and yet your momentum may have lulled you into a state of complacency and familiarity. In that case, doing something new can easily be dismissed—especially if it's an unusual technique. So let's refute the common arguments you could use to talk yourself out of trying or maintaining this practice:

- *It's too easy.* Some people think that something so simple can't have a beneficial effect, yet every case cited in this book is true, and these are just a few of the great responses I've heard about.

- *It's too complicated.* Interestingly enough, I also hear that it's too complex to learn or perhaps to keep up. This may be so at the beginning, but once you get into the swing of things, it becomes spontaneous, natural, and quick.

- *I'm too busy.* When someone runs from task to task, they often don't want to take the time to start something new. Yes, there may be some initial time investment when you're investigating your reactive patterns and designing your decoding and coding statements. After that, it's just a few minutes a day. No matter how busy you are, you'll find that your quick coding sessions will create and sustain a happy, self-empowered life.

- *I don't trust it (or believe in it).* Doubt and suspicion have become a way of life for many people. Some try the technique once or twice and then give up, and some don't even try it at all. Yet the efficacy is undeniable when dealing with so many types of issues. Plus it makes you feel so good! So give it a try and keep on using it. Don't give up! Every time you shift your energy, you redirect the destiny of your life.

If any of these objections have come to your mind, let yourself break free of your hesitation. Decode any doubt or resistance, and code an openness and willingness to change. As time goes on, let yourself become more conscious of when you have the option to do the technique, and make that choice a priority.

It's especially necessary to repeat the technique when you're dealing with deeply embedded longings, attachments, and negative thought patterns. Yet for some reason, it's during the difficult times that people tend to resist the most. Defy the resistance, and when you're feeling overwhelmed, take some time to set this new energy and thought change in motion. When you feel any resistance or discouragement, just take a deep breath, and in the postures say, *I decode resistance; I decode doubt and let it go. I code peace in the process. I am free.*

No matter what you're going through, you can still insert this change into your life and reclaim your power at any time. It may take some repetition, but it does make a difference if you remember to do it. In fact, there are many quick and easy things that you can do to shift your patterns into bright, new codes, including using the coding position for affirmations, visualization, and something I call *tidbit coding.*

Tidbit Coding

There are lots of little, easy activities that can integrate the coding technique into your daily life. One is what I call *tidbit coding.* This is where you have *a simple item that you want to change, so you take just a few seconds to do so at the time of the activity.* This usually involves coding an emotional quality to an experience—oftentimes it's adding comfort or excitement to something that you find uncomfortable or unsatisfactory. It could even be an activity you do all the time, yet never have thought of coding to be more joyful. Let's look at an example.

Emma, the woman who was working on losing weight, was decoding her escapism and food addiction, but she was also approaching her weight-loss intention on several levels. One of them was to sign up at a local gym and get a trainer. Emma did most of what the trainer asked without any hesitation, but she hated doing lunges. I suggested that the next time she went to the gym, she quickly code enjoyment of the exercise, along with satisfaction and fun. It took only a few seconds, but it had the desired effect.

When I talked to her a few days later, she told me that the experience had changed for her. Although she still didn't love that particular part of the routine, she didn't hate it like before. She said the time went by much faster, and she felt much more satisfaction and self-pride. She was still motivated to go to the gym and do her entire routine, and she was finally off her plateau and losing weight once again.

I use this tidbit coding whenever I'm tired or I have something to do that I'm not looking forward to. I take just a few moments to code satisfaction and even excitement about the activity, and it's amazing to see how quickly my mood shifts from dread to peace. Often, I even find myself looking forward to the experience!

So try this tidbit coding whenever you find yourself engaged in—or anticipating—an activity that doesn't thrill you. You can also do this throughout the day, using the coding posture to create joy in any task. This will renew your energy and bring a more heightened sense of satisfaction—and even excitement—around the little things in life that may have more power over your moods than you realize.

Energizing Affirmations

The coding position is also good for charging up your affirmations. Pick one or two that you can recite rapidly, and as you do so, take a deep breath and engage in the coding posture for just a few seconds. Of course, the coding statements themselves are also affirmations, so you can pick your favorites and use them throughout the day.

The emotional codes and single words of power, such as *happiness* and *peace,* are also great options for rapid-fire affirmations in the coding position. Doing these several times a day creates a wonderful energetic momentum and powerful intention. You can pick some words or phrases that you want to focus on each day or use your intuition in response to whatever may come up. Just make sure you remember to do it—and repeat it with joyous intention. Your days will flow with pleasing synchronicity, and your energy will be irresistibly sweet!

Rapid-Fire Visualization

As you know from learning about the second breakthrough force of vision, the practice of visualization can be a powerful tool in shifting your consciousness, as well as your results. The coding technique can be used to accelerate the energy of your visualizations, even if they're engaged in only for just a moment or two. Here are some scenes that you can envision:

- The successful end results of a goal you have in mind

- Images of yourself being congratulated for some personal success

- Scenes from a wonderful vacation or event you'd like to experience

- Visions of yourself happily engaging in any joyous activity

These are all visualizations relating to your desires and goals, whether emotional, financial, or relationship. But you can also visualize little wisps of memory where you had a happy experience or enjoyed a specific place, person, or event. These visions create an emotional oasis and dynamic shifts in consciousness as well. So let yourself take a few moments each day to use the coding position to picture something such as the following:

- Looking out at your favorite vacation spot

- A happy memory when you were engaged in pleasant activity

- A time when you were happy and connecting with someone you care about

- A silly joke or funny scene that makes you smile or laugh

Simply pick any item on either of these lists, engage in the posture, and take a deep breath. All you need to do is hold the fingertips of your right hand to your forehead for just a few moments as you fill in the details of this joyous vision. Let yourself smile and then immediately disconnect the position, dropping your hands as you relax and hold the picture in your mind for just a few minutes longer. Take a deep breath and release the image to the Universe, and let yourself continue to bask in the joyous energy that you felt while engaged in that wonderful vision of yours.

You can bring comfort, happiness, fun, or excited optimism to any moment. Charge each day with quick and simple coding. Your choice to do so will connect the energies of present appreciation with joyous expectation, creating a vortex of beautiful resonance that moves from your heart and mind out into the world.

CHAPTER 18

THE HEART OF HAPPINESS

"Deep within you is everything that is perfect,
ready to radiate through you and out into the world."

— *The Course in Miracles*

It may seem as though we've been dealing only with issues of the mind, and of course that's where the focus of this energy is. But I believe that ultimately the decoding gets us out of our heads, and the coding gets us into our hearts. After all, the head is where all our mental patterns reside, and the heart is where the feelings of freedom, love, and courage are born.

You see, it's the job of the mind to *judge* value, whereas the heart *experiences* it. The mind just gets on a treadmill of unending analysis with thoughts like *Is that good for me? Am I good enough? What if this doesn't happen? What if that does?*

These and so many other analytical judgments are just a part of a whole network of unwanted reactive patterns. The decoding process helps get us out of this mental analysis and moves us into the experience of value instead. Every time we code things such as peace, trust, or freedom, we get off the treadmill that takes us nowhere and move into the heart-centered consciousness of present value and peace.

There's another easy posture that can facilitate this as well. I call it the *Peace Process,* and you can do it by itself or add this little practice to the end of your coding experience.

The Peace Process

Do you remember when you were a little kid and you used to do a *pinky swear* to make a heart-to-heart promise with a friend? In that process, you would hook your little finger to a friend's little finger and shake on some sort of agreement. Well, I don't know how or when this sweet ceremony got started, but it shows the delightful insight and intuition of childhood. The little fingers are at the end of the heart meridians, the lines of energy that are vibrationally connected with the fourth—or heart—center, the perfect place for a sincere intention.

In fact, the heart chakra is a powerful place for shifting your core vibration. The more you get out of turbulent mental analysis and move your consciousness into the calm and loving energy of the heart, the more peaceful, productive, and happy you will be.

It takes conscious awareness to let go of the pattern of constant worry that only keeps attracting more things to worry about. But there's also an easy little process that can quiet your mind and very quickly bring you real feelings of peace. Like the specifics of the coding technique, I was given the details of this position in a dream—just a few days after the first one.

It's a process that's so simple, it was hard for me to believe that it could be so effective. But after teaching it to hundreds of people, I've found it to be utterly amazing. (It seems that the simplest things can often be the most profound.) So open your heart and get ready to be at peace!

The Peace Process starts by linking the little fingers of your own two hands together. Just allow yourself to sit in a comfortable position, take a deep breath, and hook one little finger around the other (as if you were making a pinky swear with yourself). Take another deep breath, and on the exhale, close your eyes and let all other thoughts go. Keeping your eyes closed, raise them up just a bit. Don't strain or stress them; just raise them slightly, keeping your little fingers hooked.

This creates a circle (actually, a heart shape) that runs energy through your heart center, down one arm, and up the other. Let yourself start to sense the current moving through you and opening your heart chakra to its perfect, healthy state.

You may not feel much at first, except perhaps for the absence of any emotion. Don't analyze what's going on. In fact, don't force yourself to think anything or code anything at all. Just let your consciousness drop into your heart center, where you can let go, relax, and open yourself to peace.

Continue to hold your fingers in position for just a little while longer, and you will soon find a greater sense of peace coming over you. After just a few moments, relax your eyes and let go of the position. Take a deep breath and allow yourself to linger in that calm and tranquil sensation. Even if you were worrying just a few minutes before you started this process, you will find that you'll feel much more peaceful, unconflicted, and calm. In fact, many people have told me that they just can't worry while engaged in this posture.

Linking to Happiness

It may seem hard to believe, but even if you spend only 20 to 30 seconds doing this process, you are making the choice to shift your consciousness. You have stepped out of analysis and stepped into heart-centered peace. Sure, it may not have solved all the problems you were anxious about, but it helps you remember that they don't have to run your life—and that worry never solves them anyway.

The bottom line is that you have far more creativity, spontaneity, and power when you're peaceful than when you're worried. And if you were to practice this little process just a few times each day, that power of peace would charge your life with a beautiful sense of well-being.

Whenever I teach this technique, people are surprised by how something so easy can automatically make them feel calm and unconcerned. One client would use it just before he asked a woman on a date (or when he caught himself brooding about asking someone out). He had been getting so agitated and desperate that his own urgent energy would push women away. But he found that the new inner peace made him far less desperate, and he was genuinely unattached to the outcome. He felt calmer, so his demeanor was personally and energetically more attractive. He decoded desperation, coded present happiness and peace, and added this heart-centered activity. He soon felt a deepening self-love, and the women he encountered were more loving and accepting as well.

I was on the phone one day with a client who was dealing with enormous hostility at work. We did the process, spending a few minutes decoding fear and powerlessness around the people involved, and then coding comfort, confidence, and personal power. I suggested he follow that up with this Peace Process, and when he did, he was amazed. He kept saying, "Oh, wow!" over and over. I asked him what he was feeling, and he said that he felt utter and complete peace. But more than that, he was seeing light all around him, even though his eyes were shut. He went to work the next day with a completely different attitude, standing up for himself and peacefully taking his power back.

So try this oh-so-easy technique whenever you find yourself worried or stressed out about something. Even if you aren't working on specific issues that cause you concern, stop at least a few times a day and make a pinky-swear promise to bring more peace to your life—and more loving energy. Do it for just a moment after coding to give yourself an extra boost. It's a simple exercise that will make a huge difference, especially when added to your new codes.

Integrate this heart-centered habit into your daily life, and don't let yourself fall out of it. Easy things are often easy to forget, so put little notes or pictures around to remind yourself. These are icons of adjacent possibility— reminders that you *always* have the option to do something different, shift your consciousness, and send your energy in much more fluid and fulfilling directions.

Clearing Your Energy and Letting It Flow

The heart chakra focused on in the Peace Process is just one of the primary energy centers of the body, which you've learned about throughout the book. Many reactive patterns can get locked in "chakra storage," making it difficult to feel centered, balance your energy, and align yourself with the flow of Universal abundance.

You don't need to know exactly what's blocked in your energy system in order to clear your difficult issues and code freedom from any problem of the past. The following list describes the location and issues of each chakra, and gives sample decoding and coding statements related to some of the challenges. The underlined words in the coding statements can code single power states when used by themselves with the coding position.

First chakra: Root center
Location: Base of the spine
Breakthrough force: Responsibility
Issues: Survival, security, personal responsibility,
    stability (including financial)

STATEMENTS	
I decode insecurity.	I code a strong sense of security.
I decode instability.	I code stability.
I decode resistance to responsibility.	I code personal responsibility.
I decode victimization.	I code personal power.
I decode depression.	I code joy and peace.

Second chakra: Sacral center
Location: Above the root center, near the sexual organs

Breakthrough force: Action
Issues: Inactivity, sexual issues, intimacy, creativity

STATEMENTS	
I decode hopelessness.	I code hope and happiness.
I decode the need to escape.	I code comfort and conscious choices.
I decode blocks to creativity.	I code creativity.
I decode fear of intimacy.	I code comfort with intimacy.
I decode fear of action.	I code a willingness to act.
I decode scattered energy.	I code focus and purpose.
I decode distraction.	I code action every day.

Third chakra: Solar plexus
Location: Above the navel, below the sternum
Breakthrough force: Joy
Issues: Emotion, desire, life force, self-valuing,
    energetic balance

STATEMENTS	
I decode lack of purpose.	I code purpose and priority.
I decode disinterest.	I code interest in my life.
I decode boredom and dissatisfaction.	I code appreciation.
I decode worry and pessimism.	I code trust and optimism.
I decode unhappiness.	I code enthusiasm.

Fourth chakra: Heart center
Location: Midchest, at the heart
Breakthrough force: Love
Issues: Love, acceptance, forgiveness, emotional
balance, and compassion

STATEMENTS	
I decode self-judgment.	I code self-love.
I decode self-dismissal.	I code self-priority.
I decode self-criticism.	I code self-acceptance.
I decode any sense of unworthiness.	I code worthiness.
I decode competition with others.	I code compassion for myself and others.
I decode fear and negativity.	I code acceptance and love.

Fifth chakra: Throat center
Location: Center of throat
Breakthrough force: Expression
Issues: Communication with self and others,
self-expression, speaking your truth

STATEMENTS	
I decode patterns of negative self-talk.	I code positive self-talk.
I decode fear of confrontation.	I code comfort in communication.
I decode patterns of shutting down.	I code new patterns of opening up.
I decode fear of self-expression.	I code ease of expression.

I decode resistance to standing up for myself.	I code the <u>ability to stand up for myself</u>.
I decode fear and refusal to risk.	I code <u>freedom</u> and <u>openness</u>.

Sixth chakra: Brow
Location: On the forehead, slightly above and
　　between the eyebrows
Breakthrough force: Vision
Issues: Insight, personal vision, clarity of thought,
　　self-view

STATEMENTS	
I decode lack of direction.	I code <u>personal direction</u>.
I decode negative self-view.	I code a <u>wonderful self-view</u>.
I decode negative views of my future.	I code a <u>beautiful view of my future</u>.
I decode lack of vision.	I code <u>purpose</u> and <u>vision</u>.
I decode views of limitation.	I code views of <u>unlimited abundance</u>.
I decode lack of clarity.	I code <u>clarity</u> and <u>insight</u>.

Seventh chakra: Crown center
Location: The top of head
Breakthrough force: Spirit
Issues: Intuition, Spirit connection, higher self,
　　higher power

STATEMENTS	
I decode lack of faith.	I code ever-deepening <u>faith</u>.
I decode any inability to relax.	I code the ability to let go and <u>relax</u>.
I decode resistance to meditation.	I code <u>comfort with meditation</u>.
I decode agitation and conflict.	I code <u>calmness</u> and <u>peace</u>.
I decode fear of Spiritual pursuits.	I code <u>comfort with Spirit presence</u>.
I decode resistance to Spirit.	I code an <u>openness</u> to <u>receive</u>.

You can use any variation of these statements to help clear old codes and stuck patterns from your energy centers. Use your intuition to address any of the issues that may be problems for you. You can also use the coding position to accelerate the following intention: *Powerful, vital energy is flowing through me now. My chakras are open to their perfect, healthy, vibrant state. I am free, flowing, and aligned with the blessings and beauty of the Universe.* Name the specific energy center that may be connected to the issue you're dealing with. For example, if you're working on being comfortable speaking up, you can say: *My throat chakra is open to its perfect, healthy, vibrant state. I am free to speak—and comfortable with expression.*

Moving On and Finding the Answers

Although the process of decoding and coding is easy once you get it going, a lot of questions or concerns may come up while you're on your way. After teaching this for a few years, I've found that people want to "do it right," but don't let this attitude stop you cold. Let yourself experiment with the technique and find your own comfort level. In case you do have any concerns, however, here are some answers to the most common questions that I've been asked.

Question: What's the most important part of the technique?

Answer: Deep breathing, the finger position, and the raised eyes seem to be the most important pieces of the puzzle, but don't make yourself crazy over any one of these details. Take your time and practice the technique. You'll get the hang of it, and your comfort level will increase. If you have a problem with *any* part of the process, don't give it up entirely. Just use your intuition and *do what you need to do* to keep your new intentions in play. Don't worry that it won't work if you have to do it a little differently. Honoring yourself is always the best approach.

Question: What if I can't raise my eyes or can't keep them raised?

Answer: Some people find that their eyes drop automatically. If this happens to you, that's fine. Rest them for a while, continue saying your statements, and just gently raise them whenever you feel comfortable doing so. Your eyes don't have to be held in an extreme position. If it's easier, just look up slightly when you're saying the statement, and then relax them on the deep breath between each directive. If your eyes drop and you don't realize it right away, don't worry. Keep doing the process and gently remind yourself to gaze upward. Do what is most comfortable for you.

Question: What if I get a headache?

Answer: You may feel some tension around the eyes or forehead, but it should go away quickly. If you notice yourself getting headaches, do shorter practices of the decoding and coding, and give yourself longer breaks between each experience. Do *not* complete more than one or two minutes at a time if you have this reaction, and give yourself at least an hour or two before doing it again. In time you'll be able to code more often with less discomfort. But remember, there's no hurry. If you do it too often because you're desperate, not only will you tense the muscles around the eyes, you'll also block the energy process as well.

Question: What if I can't remember my statements while I'm doing the process?

Answer: This is a common issue and can happen whenever you choose a new pattern to work on. Let yourself form easier statements at first, or choose to do just one or two phrases at a time. If you need to, you can have your statements written out in front of you and take a moment to look at each one before you move on. You can also record your statements to help you through the process. With more and more practice, you'll remember what you're working on. If memory fails, use a simple phrase that comes to mind. Let your intuition lead you in the right direction.

Question: What if I miss a few days—or even longer? Will it still work?

Answer: If you're like me, you'll miss plenty of days. Whenever you get busy or stressed out, this little process that can keep you calm and focused is often the first thing to go. Don't worry about this. People who have made permanent changes—like quitting smoking and learning to be happy—have been able to maintain the shift. Yet they find it very helpful to repeat the process whenever they notice any old longing or other negative pattern come up. Sometimes you just have to remind yourself to do it—even if everything is going well. There's always more joy and peace to code, and doing this coding is a wonderful way of life!

Question: What if I don't notice anything?

Answer: Most people notice some physical sensations, such as tingling, buzzing, or feeling light-headed, while they are doing the process itself. If you don't have these, it doesn't mean that the process isn't working. Just let yourself continue to use it and see what happens. You may never have a physical sensation, but that's okay.

Most people also feel at least a little improvement in their energy or emotion immediately after doing the coding technique. For others, the personal responses are far subtler and take more time. Jotting down a few quick notes in your coding journal is invaluable in tracking this information. If you don't have any emotional shifts, it may be because you're feeling desperate about the issue or searching for something to happen. This desperation and self-scrutiny take away your peaceful approach and make it difficult for the experience to be felt. Decode any desperation, and code a relaxed approach instead. Let yourself continue to do the process without too much scrutiny and examination. Your effects will become more and more noticeable over time.

Question: What if I have some physical limitations and can't lift my hands to my head or raise my eyes?

Answer: Always honor what is most comfortable for you. If you can't perform the physical parts of the process, do the rest of the technique along with the deep breathing as described. You can also just visualize yourself touching your forehead or raising your eyes as if they were in the position physically. Direct your subconscious mind to know or sense that the technique is being done effectively anyway. Trust this to be so.

Question: Can the technique be used to heal physical problems?

Answer: I taught the technique at a seminar in which one of the participants told me about her persistent and severe migraine headaches. That week, she used the process as soon as a migraine was starting to set in, and found that the pain quickly went away, saving her hours or even days of suffering. However, the real focus of this process is to release and reverse mental, emotional, and energetic patterns. Of course, things like weight loss and quitting smoking have major physical components, but I have never used it to change a physical condition such as arthritis or diabetes. But you may want to give it a try, and I'd be interested in finding out how it goes.

Marina's Open Heart

I recently received an e-mail from a lovely lady named Marina who wanted to tell me about her experience. She had been doing the decoding and coding, focusing on the energy of love, so she decided to do the heart chakra Peace Process seven times in one day. She was working on clearing self-criticism and coding worthiness and self-love, all issues she had built reactive patterns around as a result of severely negative input from her ex.

During the seven repetitions of the Peace Process, she had many realizations in which she felt a strong release and reprogramming taking place, including feeling the shift of her own voice from one of negativity into one of self-compassion. She now knew that what she heard in her own voice was her own choice.

Another very interesting event took place for Marina on that heart-opening day. Several months earlier, she had been in a car accident for which she'd been blamed. That day she received a check in the mail along with a letter assigning responsibility to the other driver, who had actually been at fault. Marina was immensely relieved and happy at this turn of events.

This is not an uncommon result, however. When you create a new code of self-love, the outer world responds in kind.

Peggy's P.S.

Throughout this book I have mentioned Peggy's trials and transformations—and her incredible shift in personal power. Since she was at the beginning of it all, I thought it only fitting to follow up on her case here at the end of the book.

I spoke to her today, and she was filled with enthusiasm and excitement about the direction her life has taken. On the professional level, she had gone from being a sales person who was nervous about taking meetings to an executive who has orchestrated large conferences.

She told me, "In some ways I feel like a child, learning how to be really happy for the first time in my life. I can be with anybody and hold my own. I feel genuinely powerful like never before!"

Her joy was palpable. Before, she had always looked to others for her good feelings, but now she was the one taking control. She was starting life brand-new—this time with a true understanding of her value and personal power. Although she had her ups and downs, whenever she returned to the process, she would invariably find herself breaking through to the next level. And now she is the person she has always longed to be, happy, powerful, and peaceful in the present.

Moments of Momentum

Remember your intention for happiness, and don't get too bogged down in the details. Everything exists in consciousness first, and you are always in the business of consciousness creation. Your thoughts and feelings create a life-force momentum that drives you forward to your destiny.

So you need to ask yourself, *How do I feel right now? Am I choosing my emotional experience or just allowing it to happen?* Decide to become more conscious of what you're doing to and with yourself. Always know that you have a choice to stop, to switch, to visualize, to choose peace, to code, to act.

You can use any present moment to decode your old patterns and formulate a new code of genuine self-empowerment and happiness. Remember to code more smiles and laughter, and also code a spiritual point of view as your automatic response to the situations you may find yourself in. All these are lifestyle changes that bring clear and calm energies to your life.

Give yourself time. Sometimes the major shifts arrive unnoticed, and you don't realize how far you've come until you look back and see how much things have changed. So *be willing to engage in this process as often as you need to and for however long it takes.* It's amazing how just a few well-placed moments repeated throughout the day can change how you feel about yourself, your life, and everything around you. It's so significant that it's worth creating the intention to make this practice a part of your routine for the rest of your life—a daily spiritual vitamin you take to build your immunity to difficulty and boost your levels of joy.

When you do this every day, you will feel the resonance of your real and authentic value and worthiness growing within you, filling you with happiness and hope—and confidence about yourself and about your ability to forge the future you desire. And when your happy resonance vibrates outward, the Universe responds accordingly. Your new code will automatically ignite joy and amazement within you, and you will soon be amazed at the wonderful experiences of your life.

Your life will be filled with synchronicity, that magical pattern where things just seem to be going your way. This is actually an energetic entrainment with the workings of the world. It aligns you with all the wonderful blessings that the Universe has to offer, and as you continue to code the love, joy, and gratitude you truly deserve, your brightening energy will keep receiving even brighter results.

We are all works in progress; and when we work on ourselves, we progress. So let yourself incorporate these new self-directed moments into your daily activities. You're going to get from here to the future anyway. You could end up in precisely the same place, experiencing the same old unwanted patterns. Or you could create a new code, a bright, new vibrational identity that radiates brilliant self-love, happiness, and deserving every day.

Your life will always reflect your choice to use and live in your own true power. These are the times for you to declare to yourself—and to the Universe—that you are in charge. Use the Quantum Breakthrough Code to take control. Keep decoding whatever may be blocking you, and never stop coding peace, release, personal power, and joy. Always remember that you have the option to use any present moment to redirect your future.

Every breakthrough force is already vibrating within you, ready to be engaged any time that you desire. Take responsibility for the quality of your life, and always act on your own behalf. See yourself as the wonderful, valuable being that you are, and be willing to express that truth to others. Know that the energies of love and joy are actually a part of your true nature, your inner state of being. Code these and every bright emotion you desire. A new life is waiting for you, and your Spirit is lighting the way.

ACKNOWLEDGMENTS

With deep appreciation to my dear friend Candace Pert, who always told me we are hardwired for bliss. It is certainly true!

With love to my family—Sarah Marie Klingler; Benjamin Earl Taylor, Jr.; Sharon Klingler; Vica Taylor; Jenyaa Taylor; Ethan Taylor; Devin Staurbringer; Yvonne Taylor; and Kevin and Kathryn Klingler.

Unending gratitude for the incredible people at Hay House, including Louise Hay, Reid Tracy, Margarete Nielsen, Christy Salinas, Jessica Kelley, Nancy Levin, Donna Abate, Shannon Godwin, Anna Almanza, Richelle Zizian, Laurel Weber, Molly Langer, Tricia Breidenthal, Wioleta Giramek, Shay Lawry, Erin Dupree, and *all* the other lovely men and women at this wonderful publishing company. And so very much appreciation to the phenomenal team at HayHouse Radio.com®, including Diane Ray, Kyle Thompson, Mitch Wilson, Joe Bartlett, and Rocky George III. You're the best!

For their tireless effort and support, Rhonda Lamvermeyer, Melissa Matousek, Lucy Dunlap, Andrea Loushine, and Cheri Polk. Thank you!

For the images in Chapters 8 and 9, much love and appreciation to Joanna Van Rensselaer.

So much appreciation to my inspiring colleagues: Gregg Braden, Bruce Lipton, Darren Weissman, Denise Linn, Lisa

Williams, Donna Eden, David Feinstein, Peggy Rometo, John Holland, Colette Baron-Reid, and Peggy McColl.

To the family of my heart—Marilyn Verbus; Barbara Van Rensselaer; Ed Conghanor; Linda Smigel; Julianne Stein; Carmine and Marie Romano; Melissa Matousek; Tom and Ellie Cratsley; Karen and Dennis Petcak; Valerie Darville; Esther Jalylatie; and Dolores, Donna, and Kathy Maroon— so much love to you all.

To my spirit family—Anna and Charles Salvaggio, Ron Klingler, Rudy Staurbringer, Earl Taylor, Chris Cary, Pat Davidson, Flo Bolton, Flo Becker, Tony, Raphael, Jude, and of course the Divine Consciousness that lives in all things and loves in all ways.

Finally, I want to thank *you* so very much—all of you who have shared your beautiful energy and support in so many ways and have brought so very much value to my life! It is my wish that the techniques in this book bring you the kind of happiness and empowerment they have brought my clients and me. I would love to hear about your results. May your life be blessed with unceasing joy!

ABOUT THE AUTHOR

Sandra Anne Taylor is the *New York Times* best-selling author of several titles including *Quantum Success,* which receives worldwide acclaim for its enlightening and comprehensive approach to the field of attraction and achievement. Rich in practical application and easy-to-understand principles, *Quantum Success* has been called "the real science of consciousness creation," and has been applauded by scientists, businessmen, and worldwide leaders in the field of consciousness dynamics for its eye-opening information and powerful strategies.

Sandra's first title, *Secrets of Attraction,* written more than 20 years ago, was the first contemporary book to reveal the influence of the Universal Laws on the pursuit of love and romance. *Truth, Triumph, and Transformation* examines the myriad influences on attraction, clearing out the fears and negativity that have recently become a common reaction to the Universal Laws. *Secrets of Success,* co-authored with Sharon Anne Klingler, explores the holistic and spiritual nature of attraction and manifestation.

The beautiful deck of *Energy Oracle Cards* helps you identify and predict energy patterns and future results in your life. Sandra's most recent book, *The Hidden Power of Your Past Lives,* explores the influence of past-life experiences on present-life patterns. *28 Days to a More Magnetic Life* is a handy, pocket-sized book that offers daily techniques and affirmations to help anyone shift their energy and create greater happiness and magnetism on a regular basis. Her many popular books are available in 26 languages across the globe.

For more than 25 years, Sandra has been a counselor in a private psychology practice, working with individuals and couples in the treatment of anxiety, depression, addiction, and relationship issues. Her Quantum Life Coaching program offers powerful techniques for connecting spirit, mind, and manifestation. Her multidimensional approach brings exceptional clarity and practicality to the science of whole-life healing and personal achievement. Sandra lives in northern Ohio with her husband and two adopted Russian-born children. Her popular radio show, *Living Your Quantum Success,* can be heard Mondays on HayHouseRadio.com®.

Sandra co-founded (along with Sharon A. Klingler) Starbringer Associates, a speaker and consultant agency that produces events and audio seminars for personal, spiritual, and business enhancement. For more information—or to schedule lectures, seminars, or business or private consultations with Sandra—contact her at:

Sandra Anne Taylor
P.O. Box 362
Avon, OH 44011
www.sandrataylor.com
facebook.com/sandraannetaylor

or

Starbringer Associates
871 Canterbury Rd., Unit B
Westlake, OH 44145
440-871-5448
www.starbringerassociates.com

Hay House Titles of Related Interest

YOU CAN HEAL YOUR LIFE, the movie,
starring Louise Hay & Friends
(available as a 1-DVD program and an expanded 2-DVD set)
Watch the trailer at: www.LouiseHayMovie.com

THE SHIFT, the movie,
starring Dr. Wayne W. Dyer
(available as a 1-DVD program and an expanded 2-DVD set)
Watch the trailer at: www.DyerMovie.com

AWAKENING TO THE SECRET CODE OF YOUR MIND: Your Mind's
Journey to Inner Peace, by Dr. Darren R. Weissman

E³: Nine More Energy Experiments That Prove Manifesting Magic
and Miracles Is Your Full-Time Gig, by Pam Grout

LOVE YOUR ENEMIES: How to Break the Anger Habit & Be a Whole
Lot Happier, by Sharon Salzberg and Robert Thurman

POWER WORDS: Igniting Your Life with Lightning Force,
by Sharon Anne Klingler

RECOVERY 2.0: Move Beyond Addiction and Upgrade Your Life,
by Tommy Rosen

THE TAPPING SOLUTION: A Revolutionary System for
Stress-Free Living, by Nick Ortner

All of the above are available at your local bookstore,
or may be ordered by contacting Hay House (see next page).

We hope you enjoyed this Hay House book. If you'd like to receive our online catalog featuring additional information on Hay House books and products, or if you'd like to find out more about the Hay Foundation, please contact:

Hay House, Inc., P.O. Box 5100, Carlsbad, CA 92018-5100
(760) 431-7695 or (800) 654-5126
(760) 431-6948 (fax) or (800) 650-5115 (fax)
www.hayhouse.com® • www.hayfoundation.org

Published and distributed in Australia by:
Hay House Australia Pty. Ltd., 18/36 Ralph St., Alexandria NSW 2015
Phone: 612-9669-4299 • *Fax:* 612-9669-4144 • www.hayhouse.com.au

Published and distributed in the United Kingdom by: Hay House UK, Ltd.,
Astley House, 33 Notting Hill Gate, London W11 3JQ
Phone: 44-20-3675-2450 • *Fax:* 44-20-3675-2451
www.hayhouse.co.uk

Published and distributed in the Republic of South Africa by:
Hay House SA (Pty), Ltd., P.O. Box 990, Witkoppen 2068
Phone/Fax: 27-11-467-8904 • www.hayhouse.co.za

Published in India by: Hay House Publishers India,
Muskaan Complex, Plot No. 3, B-2, Vasant Kunj, New Delhi 110 070
Phone: 91-11-4176-1620 • *Fax:* 91-11-4176-1630 • www.hayhouse.co.in

Distributed in Canada by: Raincoast Books,
2440 Viking Way, Richmond, B.C. V6V 1N2 •
Phone: 1-800-663-5714 • *Fax:* 1-800-565-3770 • www.raincoast.com

Take Your Soul on a Vacation

Visit www.HealYourLife.com® to regroup,
recharge, and reconnect with your own magnificence.
Featuring blogs, mind-body-spirit news, and
life-changing wisdom from Louise Hay and friends.

Visit www.HealYourLife.com today!